T5-BQA-506

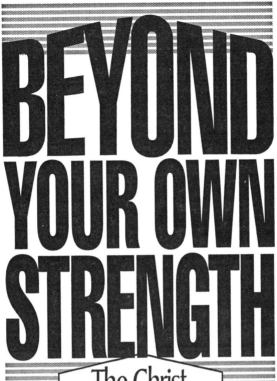

BEYOND YOUR OWN STRENGTH

The Christ-
Empowered
Life

FRANK DAMAZIO

Creation House
Lake Mary, Florida

Creation House
Strang Communications Company
600 Rinehart Road
Lake Mary, FL 32746
(407) 333-0600

Unless otherwise noted, all Scripture references are taken from the New American Standard Bible; copyright © 1960, 1962, 1963, 1968, 1971, 1972, 1973, 1975, 1977, by the Lockman Foundation; used by permission.

Lyrics from "A Mighty Fortress Is Our God" by Martin Luther are used with permission from Augsburg-Fortress Publishers, Minneapolis, Minn.

To Mathew Madathil,
a fellow minister who labored
together with me in the gospel and
exemplified a "beyond your own
strength" spirit

CONTENTS

Yes,
I Can...

1 ■ Be a Winner!....................11

2 ■ Be Courageous!....................27

3 ■ Possess God's Promises!....................39

4 ■ Be Motivated!....................53

5 ■ Have a Living Faith!....................69

6 ■ Be a Rejoicing Christian!....................79

7 ■ Be a Harvester!....................93

8 ■ Be a Godly Father!....................107

9 ■ Keep on Keepin' On!....................123

10 ■ Live Out My Dreams!....................139

Notes....................153

Yes,
I Can...

Be a
Winner!

ONE

Did you know that bumblebees can't fly? That's right. According to the principles of aeronautics, the shape and weight of their bodies in relation to their total wing area make it impossible for bumblebees to fly. Fortunately, however, bumblebees don't know anything about the principles of aeronautics. So they just go ahead and fly anyway!

Maybe it's the same way with you. Maybe life has crippled you—or so you've been told. Maybe you're a loser—or so you've been told.

But maybe what you've been told isn't the way it

needs to be. Maybe you can be like the bumblebee. Ignore what "they" say. Just go ahead and fly anyway!

Decide to Be a Winner

Often all that separates a winner from a loser is the decision to be a winner. And only you can decide to win. You can win when others lose and soar when others sink. You've been called to be a winner! I want to challenge you to become a winner in a world of quitters and losers.

Your natural birth, your circumstances and what others have told you don't determine whether or not you'll be a winner. Winning is a matter of your decision. Right now you can decide to become one of God's winners in this life, in your circumstances, right where you live.

You can be a champion, a valiant fighter, gaining superiority over all the enemies that would hold you down. You can be a conqueror and more than a conqueror, overcoming all forces that come up against you with overwhelming victory. You can be a winner!

Challenges or Opportunities?

Life continually brings circumstances that try to hold you down. Lies of the enemy come against your mind, trying to tell you that you can never be a winner, a champion. But the Bible is the final court of appeal. The Bible is the answer to every lie and accusation of the devil. And the Bible teaches that you have everything you need to rise above your circumstances, overcome your handicaps and be a winner now! "In all these things we overwhelmingly conquer through him who loved us" (Rom. 8:37).

Many people live day-to-day full of worry, fear and doubt with mountains of problems overwhelming them. They have surrendered to lies, obstacles and circumstances. They have given up the idea that they can overcome the challenges they face and be winners.

But those challenges aren't put before us to discourage us. Challenges can remind us of our weaknesses and our need for total dependence on God. Challenges give us an opportunity to be stretched beyond our normal capacity.

Do you face some challenges today? Take heart! The Scriptures are filled with stories of men and women who had challenges before them but who came out as conquerors and overcomers. And if you apply the biblical principles they used—principles we'll examine in this book—so will you!

A Transformed Mind

To be a winner you must first change the way you think. If you think like a loser, you'll live like a loser. If you want to live like a winner, you must transform your mind into the mind of a winner.

The great judge Oliver Wendell Holmes once said, "Man's mind, stretched by a new idea, never goes back to its original dimensions." [1] God wants to stretch our minds. He wants to give us new thoughts and ideas. He wants our creativity to surface so we might be all that He has called us to be. Our full potential is lying dormant like a seed. The Holy Spirit wants to water that seed so it can break forth into new growth.

Winners open their minds to the renewing of the Holy Spirit. Are you preoccupied with the past and with things you cannot control? Is your mind filled with self-talk about what "should" have been, "could" have been or "might" have been?

Victim or Victor?

Have you been plagued with the "victim" mode of thinking? "Whatever happens, happens. There's nothing I can do about it." Are you pessimistic about your present, your past and your future?

Get rid of that kind of thinking. God hasn't called you to be a victim; He's called you to be a victor! He's called you to be like Joshua, Caleb, Daniel and David—someone who when faced with obstacles rises up and says, "Yes, I can change this situation!"

Are you plagued with the "maintainer" mode of thinking? Preoccupied with the present view of reality and present needs? Do you do just enough to get by? Are you always doing what's safe—what's guaranteed to work? Do you find you have no faith to reach forward, to stretch, to take risks?

Such a mind-set will hinder your growth. You're not called simply to exist in a safe environment. You're called to reach out of your comfort zone, take risks and move forward!

Or are you one with a "someday" kind of thinking: "I know what I'll do...someday"? But do you have any concrete plans for fulfilling your vision? Have you taken any steps toward implementing those plans?

None of these ways of thinking is for winners. We will not be victims. We will not just maintain. We will not settle for what's safe. We will become winners!

Make It Happen!

Winners change the way they think. Their thinking becomes adventurous! Winners don't merely react to change; they create change. Winners make things happen. Like Joshua and Caleb, they say, "We should by all means go up and take possession of [the land], for we shall surely overcome" (Num. 13:30).

You and I are winners—if we choose to be. We are more than able to do what God has called us to do. We have the spirit of Joshua and Caleb. We can learn to see opportunity in everything. We can learn to see value in everything. Nothing can keep us down. Nothing can turn us into negative people. Nothing can control our attitudes. We control them through the confession of our mouths:

"Yes, I can conquer! Yes, I can change! Yes, God has called me to be a winner!" Thoughts like these bring the Holy Spirit into action in our lives.

If you find yourself going in circles; if you're bored; if you've created a rut in your life—set yourself free right now by allowing the Holy Spirit to transform your thinking. Climb out of "thinking ruts" that stifle productivity: the rut of conventional wisdom; the rut of group thinking; the rut of what everybody else thinks about you; the rut of what the spirit of the day is saying.

In his letter to the Romans Paul insisted: "Do not be conformed to this world, but be transformed by the renewing of your mind" (12:2). This passage can also be rendered, "Be transformed by your new attitude of mind" or "Continue to transform yourselves by the new ideas that mold your mind." You don't have to wait for success. It's waiting for you in God's Word.

Mental Training

Did you know you can train yourself to think better? You can escape ruts by trying out new possibilities. For example, list ten ways of doing the impossible. This will give you a new perspective on whatever obstacle is confronting you. Stand back and look at things from a distance; list some ways you can work through a problem. Imagine what could happen if you removed the "I can't" attitude and replaced it with "Yes, I can!"

While reading 1 Corinthians 13:4-7, the famous passage about love, a friend of mine named Walt was inspired by a visionary idea for overcoming self-sabotaging habits of anger and selfishness. He decided to memorize this passage day by day for thirty days. Walt would meditate upon these verses over and over:

Love is patient, love is kind, and is not jealous; love does not brag and is not arrogant, does not act unbecomingly; it does not seek its own, is not provoked, does not take into account a wrong suffered, does not rejoice in unrighteousness, but rejoices with the truth; bears all things, believes all things, hopes all things, endures all things.

As he repeated the Word of God daily, he was amazed at how he began to relax and turn his thoughts toward ways of demonstrating the very words he was speaking. Those of us who saw Walt change could not refute the power of God's Word displayed before our very eyes.

All of us need a transformation of our minds. We need some new ideas and new thinking patterns that will bring us into a winner's way of living. We're not called to be losers; we're called to be conquerors.

Problems or Challenges?

King David is a great biblical example of a winner. He embodied four important attitudes of winners:

1. Winners respond to the challenge, not the problem. In 1 Samuel 17:23-27 we read how David faced Goliath, a ten-foot giant who had been trained for war since his youth. Goliath had a breastplate that weighed two hundred pounds and a spear that was eight feet long. The head of the spear alone was twenty-five pounds of iron! This fearsome warrior had been challenging the armies of God for forty days and forty nights.

Nevertheless, David didn't see Goliath as a problem. He saw him as a challenge. He saw a man who was challenging God's faithfulness to His people, who was trusting in false gods, defying the one true God. Because David had a winner's perspective, he was able to rise up against his problem—Goliath—and slay him with the help of God. He knew that God was greater than his problem.

How Will You Respond?

Why do some win and others lose? Why do some soar and others sink? It depends on how you perceive your problem and how you perceive your God. Like David, you must learn to put your problems into proper perspective. That means allowing the Holy Spirit to show you that the problem is not really the problem! The real problem lies in challenging God's ability and faithfulness.

Everyone has problems. No one is exempt. Every problem will affect us. We may not be able to prevent problems or even control the timing. But we can control our response. We can turn our pain into either poetry or profanity. Unwanted pregnancy, financial problems, marital problems, church problems, drug and alcohol problems, unemployment—how will you respond? Will you run, hide and make excuses? Or will you face the problems that are challenging your God, remembering that God will rise to the occasion?

Who Cares What "They" Say?

2. Winners don't allow themselves to be shaped by circumstances, criticisms or the opinions of others. In 1 Samuel 17:28-33 we're told that Eliab, David's older brother, tried to deflate David's champion attitude into a defeatist attitude. He tried to embarrass David and belittle him and to tear down any sense of success or importance David may have had.

He even questioned David's integrity and motives: "I know the pride and foolishness of your heart, your forwardness and self-will. This is nothing more than your old self-conceit, the old cunning character I've seen before. Into whose care have you given that little flock of sheep in the wasteland?" Like Eliab, the devil always comes in to tear you down, to insert doubt in your mind, to make you feel powerless and hopeless.

Saul, too, attacked David: "You're not able; you're far too young. You won't be able to take on this Philistine. You'll die!"

Many people are overly influenced by what other people think of them and say to them—parents, friends, teachers, even complete strangers. But that can lead to trouble, because people will question your motives based on their own wrong motives. People will judge your ambitions by their own insecurities. They will judge after the flesh, the human mind, the eye of human reason, and say, "You can't."

But God judges after the spirit, the eternal mind, and says in His Word that *you can* do what He has called you to do: "From now on we recognize no man according to the flesh" (2 Cor. 5:16); "God has chosen the weak things of the world to shame the things which are strong" (1 Cor. 1:27); "When I am weak, then I am strong" (2 Cor. 12:10). The Lord sees "not as man sees, for man looks at the outward appearance, but the Lord looks at the heart" (1 Sam. 16:7).

These Scripture passages should cause you to take heart when those around you try to shape your attitudes negatively, criticizing you and giving you their wrong opinions of what you're trying to do.

Stand on God's Word

3. Winners live by what God's Word says, not by what they see, hear or imagine to be true. Look at these verses in 1 Samuel 17: Goliath "stood and *shouted*" (v. 8); "the Philistine [Goliath] *said*" (v. 10); "Israel heard these *words*" (v. 11); and

"Goliath...*spoke* these same *words*; and David heard them" (v. 23). A battle was going on before David even took up his sling, and it was a battle of words—Goliath's words versus God's word.

David could have responded to the words he was hearing from an uncircumcised Philistine. But David also had a word from God, and with that word he stood. It was the word of the covenant, a word that God would never leave him or forsake him. David's stand was based on his knowledge of God and God's word.

Pope Gregory I said, "The words of God you receive by your ear, hold fast in your heart, for the word of God is the food of the soul." What word has God recently planted in your heart? Hold fast to it and use it to wage war against every word of the enemy. Always be on guard. When evil, negative words and thoughts come into your heart, dash them at once on the rock of Christ.

Countering Satan's Lies

Revelation 12:9-10 and Luke 4:5-6 confirm that the enemy will use lying words to tear us down. Here are twelve lies the enemy will commonly use against you, along with the twelve responses of a winner. Remember: The dynamic words of a champion will defeat the lying words of the enemy.

Destructive Words of the Enemy *(Twelve Lies of the Devil)* 1 Samuel 17:8,10,11,23 Revelation 12:9-10 Luke 4:3,5-7,9	**Dynamic Words of the Champion** *(Twelve Responses of a Champion)* Revelation 12:11 Matthew 4:4,7,10 1 Samuel 17:26,29,30,31 Ephesians 6:17 Colossians 3:16 Hebrews 4:12
1. You will never be satisfied with life. Discontentment will always be with you.	Psalm 145:16 Psalm 36:8 Jeremiah 31:14
2. You are not worthy to receive anything from God.	Luke 15:21,22,24 Psalm 103:1-5
3. You will not win this battle. The battle's too strong—you'll lose. This problem is far beyond your ability. You'll quit before the end.	1 Samuel 17:46,47 2 Chronicles 20:15 Jeremiah 32:17
4. You will never completely change. You will always have hidden habits. You're a hypocrite in life.	2 Corinthians 5:17 Philippians 1:6
5. You will always have financial problems. You're cursed with poverty; you will never get ahead.	Malachi 3:9-11 Psalm 24:5

6. You will never be loved or accepted. You're a misfit; you're unlovable. You're different.	Ephesians 1:6 1 John 4:10,11,19 Ephesians 2:4
7. You will never find the will of God. You're going to miss God's best.	Psalm 32:8 Ephesians 5:17; 6:6 Colossians 1:9 1 Thessalonians 5:18
8. You're not totally forgiven; you've done some things that will never be forgiven, never cleansed. You're a second-class citizen.	Psalm 103:3 1 John 1:9 Psalm 103:12 Isaiah 1:18
9. You have lost God's best for your life. Your birthright is gone; you will never do what God has called you to do. Your ministry is gone! You're a failure!	Jonah 3:1 Mark 16:7 2 Timothy 4:11 Micah 7:14
10. You are different. You will find God like other people. You will never be loved; you will never have a spiritual language—you may as well accept it. Just live as you are now! Intellectual doubter, your mind won't submit.	Romans 10:8-11 2 Chronicles 15:2 Jeremiah 29:13
11. You don't need God; you're strong, intelligent, self-sufficient. You're not a bad sinner. God is for the real bad people. You can live without God; you have so far. God is for the weak.	2 Corinthians 12:9,10 Hebrews 11:6 James 4:13-15 Proverbs 16:18
12. You will never be a witness; you're far too ignorant. Nobody will listen to you; you can't speak clearly. You don't know the Bible.	Acts 1:8 1 Corinthians 1:26-28 Exodus 4:10-12

Nothing Is Impossible

4. Winners respond with courage to seemingly impossible challenges. We all face great opportunities brilliantly disguised as impossible situations! Some see these great opportunities as intruders into their peaceful lives or as problems that are unsolvable, impossible or unfair. Tell me your thoughts, and I will tell you your destiny!

As David did, you face a Goliath who has come to challenge you. How will you respond? Like a wimp or a winner? As David did, you can draw on the courage of God within your spirit to rise to that challenge. Challenges are here to remind you of your weaknesses and your total dependence on God. He gives you opportunities to be stretched beyond your normal strength and abilities. We'll look at this in greater depth in the next chapter.

Yes,
I Can...

Be
Courageous!

TWO

We live in a pressure-cooker age. Alcoholism, drug abuse, child abuse, job changes, divorce—many of these problems are simply signs of people not coping with pressure. They're not rising to meet their Goliath with the courage God has made available to all of us.

Every stage of life has its pressures—even childhood and the teenage years. Suicide is on the increase among youth between the ages of thirteen and nineteen. It's even rising among young children six to eight years old. Why? Many of these young people don't know how to cope with pressure, because their parents don't know how to cope with pressure.

Newlyweds have pressures. On a stress scale of one to one hundred, just being newly married scores fifty points. Why? So many adjustments must be made: financial adjustments, career adjustments, role adjustments. Many young couples aren't prepared to rise to the challenge.

Single parents have tremendous pressures: financial challenges, loneliness, adjustments in every area of life.

We all have our Goliaths: rocky marriages, ailing mates, a handicapped child, vocational inadequacies. Yet with the courage God has for us, we can face any of these problems—and overcome them!

Run to Meet Goliath!

God doesn't give us wings to fly away from problems. He doesn't take us out of the world to keep us from experiencing pressure. Instead, He gives us the strength to walk through the pressure and to be enlarged even while we're under stress.

God allowed the three children of Israel to go into the fiery furnace, but He kept them safe. God won't always turn down the heat. But He'll always get in there with us and give us the strength to overcome whatever we face.

We can cope with problems in one of four ways: run away from them, go around them (only to face them again later), ignore them or do as David did: turn to face them with courage, knowing that God will help us overcome them. David's behavior in 1

Samuel 17:48 reflects the attitude of a winner: he *hastened* to meet Goliath.

Courage is the attitude we need when we're facing danger, difficulty or pain. Courage is the quality of standing fast instead of stepping back when facing opposition. To be courageous is to be bold, alert, firm and persistent when coming up against a Goliath. Courage isn't the absence of fear; rather it is the refusal to be mastered by fear.

As we move in the spirit of courage, we'll confront our opponent with the confidence that we'll ultimately succeed—acting as though it were impossible for us to fail. This is the way David faced Goliath. He didn't hesitate for one moment. He didn't wait for Goliath to come and meet him. He ran out to meet Goliath.

We can approach our problems in the same way. We should go out to meet them, knowing we can overcome. Joshua's words to the Israelites are for us as well: ''Be strong and courageous, for thus the Lord will do to all your enemies with whom you fight'' (Josh. 10:25).

Hitting the Mark

A story is told about Henry Ward Beecher, one of the great preachers of the American past, that he once waged a preaching campaign against gambling and drunkenness in a particular city. He spoke out so boldly that he stirred up considerable trouble in the community. One of the city's leading citizens, who happened to own the gambling casinos and was supplying the alcohol for the city's drunkenness, was going bankrupt because of Beecher's preaching. So he met Beecher on the street one day with a pistol in his hand and said, "Take back what you said, or I will shoot you on the spot."

Beecher responded: "Go ahead and shoot. I don't believe you can hit the mark as well as I did."

That's courage! That's a man who knows his God. That's a man who knows how to stand in spite of opposition.

Building Courage

What changes a wimp into a champion, a failure into a success, a shepherd into a giant killer? It's courage. "The Spirit of the Lord came mightily upon David from that day forward" (1 Sam. 16:13). The Spirit of the Lord was David's source of courage. It broke every bondage in his life. Fear fell away from David's life because of the anointing of God's Spirit.

We cultivate courage by gaining victories in the seemingly insignificant matters of daily life. We build a winner's attitude by overcoming in these small areas. In 1 Samuel 17:34-37 David said he had been keeping the sheep successfully. David began by being responsible with a few sheep, and God eventually entrusted him with the entire flock of Israel. David had built a character of courage even in the little things of life.

"Your servant has killed both the lion and the

bear," David was able to say. "The Lord delivered me out of the paw of the lion and the paw of the bear." God's acts of faithfulness in the past were fresh in David's mind. This memory built faith for the future challenges he was to face.

We, too, need to build memories of past victories— our own "museum of God's faithfulness." I have a friend who keeps a victory journal in which he logs notes of personal triumphs. His writings contain memories of goals attained, obstacles overcome and challenges conquered, as well as his feelings during and after the battles.

Re-reading these pages, which he calls "my inside story," gives him the growing assurance and stronger faith he needs to face the future. "As [a man] thinks within himself, so he is" (Prov. 23:7).

It's Always Too Soon to Quit

Is your heart discouraged today? Take heart! Understand that God is for you even in your weakness. He is for you even when you stumble. God loves you and is eager to help you right now.

A Christian college in Illinois had a watchword some years back: "Too soon to quit." Winners know that it's always too soon to quit.

If you're discouraged today, remember: It's too soon to quit. The Holy Spirit will come. He'll bring courage to your heart and cause you to be a winner. You'll be able to rise up and say, "Yes, I *am* a winner Yes, I *can* be courageous."

"Do Not Fear"

The forty-first chapter of Isaiah records several promises to a discouraged champion. Meditate on these promises. Let them seep into your spirit and encourage you.

"But you, Israel, My servant, Jacob whom I have chosen, descendant of Abraham My friend, you whom I have taken from the ends of the earth, and called from its remotest parts, and said to you, 'You are My servant, I have chosen you and not rejected you.

" 'Do not fear, for I am with you; do not anxiously look about you, for I am your God. I will strengthen you, surely I will help you, surely I will uphold you with My righteous right hand.'

"Behold, all those who are angered at you will be shamed and dishonored; those who contend with you will be as nothing, and will perish. You will seek those who quarrel with you, but will not find them, those who war with you will be as nothing, and non-existent.

"For I am the Lord your God, who upholds your right hand, who says to you, 'Do not fear, I will help you.' Do not fear, you worm Jacob, you men of Israel; I will help you," declares the Lord, "and your Redeemer is the Holy One of Israel.

"Behold, I have made you a new, sharp threshing sledge with double edges; you will thresh the mountains, and pulverize them, and will make the hills like chaff" (Is. 41:8-15).

God has given us seven important promises here:
1. "I have chosen you and not rejected you" (v. 9).

Even though Israel was in captivity and the marks of God's covenant mercy were not apparent, God reassured them, "I have not rejected you."

God reassures you today as well. Even though you may experience bondage and weakness in your life, you have not been rejected. His hand is upon you right now. He has chosen you.

2. "Do not fear, for I am with you; do not anxiously look about you" (v. 10).

You don't have to look around frantically for help as though you had to take heed for yourself. The Lord says, "I am with you even when you think you're facing life all alone."

You may feel very much alone right now. You may feel totally abandoned. But don't fear. Your God will rise to the challenge and work with you in this situation.

3. "I am your God [Elohim]" (v. 10).

"Elohim," the name of God used here, means "high and lifted up, the mighty one." We serve a mighty God. We serve an awesome God. His arm is not so short that He cannot reach out to us.

You can arise in this situation and turn your eyes

to the mighty God. The God who opened the Red Sea is the same God who stands with you today. The God who delivered Christ from the tomb is the same God who can open your situation and bring you through.

4. "I will strengthen you, surely I will help you" (v. 10).

This phrase actually means that God will make you strong by divine encounter. God is your strength. Paul says, "When I am weak, then I am strong." The Holy Spirit is coming today to make you strong and hard: not hard toward God, but hard to your difficulties so that you might be able to withstand them as a winner.

5. "I will uphold you with My righteous right hand" (v. 10).

God holds up our hands in the battle. He assures the victory. Sometimes our hands grow weary, and we feel like letting them fall to our side. But the Lord says, "I will uphold you. I will be your victory even when you don't feel like the victory is there."

6. "Those who contend with you shall be as nothing, and will perish. You will seek those who quarrel with you, but will not find them" (vv. 11-12).

Many enemies lurk around you—demonic enemies that want to harass you and steal the life of God from you. But the Lord says, "I will destroy all your enemies." And on the cross the Lord Jesus Christ bought us the victory. When Christ died and rose from the dead, He destroyed the works of the enemy, and He gives us the power to do the same.

7. "I have made you a new, sharp threshing sledge with double edges" (v. 15).

Now maybe you don't feel like a sharp threshing instrument at this point. Maybe you haven't had the attitude of a winner in your life as you'd like to have. But you need to take these promises right now and apply them to your life. The Lord promises that, if we follow Him, He'll change us and mold us into a new, sharp, threshing instrument. In the Spirit of God is an attitude of victory—the attitude of a winner!

Pulling the Load

I once heard a story about some horses drawing a heavy load of logs. They came to a hard place and began to struggle. They worked with all their might, straining every muscle to the snapping point. But they couldn't start up the hill. It was too steep, and the logs were too heavy.

The driver took some logs off the wagon and tried to get them started again, but nothing happened. The horses tried to pull the logs up the hill, but again they couldn't get started. The driver went back and rolled off more logs. Once again he prodded the horses to go up the hill. Again nothing happened. They were now so tired they couldn't take even one step forward.

At last the driver took all the logs off the wagon and prodded the horses gently. They started slowly but gained momentum until they went all the way to the top.

Lightening the Burden

Discouragement drains strength and makes light loads seem heavy. Those horses had been utterly discouraged. They had pulled with all their strength and failed. Anyone doing that, man or beast, won't be able to accomplish much.

At times, however, the Holy Spirit will come to our side and unload the logs. Sometimes He'll take off every burden. At other times He'll take only a few. But He always knows exactly how many to take off for us to regain our strength and go on.

Remember, the horses were more important than the load of logs, and you are more important to God than the burdens you're carrying right now. Let the Lord unload some of them from your life so you can fan to life again your spirit of courage and move forward.

Say to yourself every day, "Yes, I _can_ be a winner. Yes, I _can_ win over discouragement. Yes, I _can_ pull those logs with all my strength. And, yes, I _can_ let some logs go. Yes, I _can_ be courageous by God's grace."

Yes,
I Can...

Possess
God's
Promises!

THREE

My daughter Nicole is seven years old. Like most seven-year-olds, Nicole is inquisitive. She also has a remarkable ability to memorize Scripture, poems, books, cartoons or anything else her little mind happens to come across.

Among the things Nicole remembers especially well are the promises I make to her. Just the other day she reminded me that I had promised to take her somewhere—and that I had never broken a promise to her. I honestly had forgotten what I'd said to her. But she let me know that my promise was her expectation.

I'm careful as a father not to break my word to my children. Building trust in children is one of the most important things a parent can accomplish, because as children learn to trust the authority of those over them they can more easily trust God and His authority. As my children learn they can believe in my promises, they'll be better able to believe in God's promises.

The Great Promise-Maker

All God's promises are in written form in His Word, the Bible, which is the authentic revelation of the divine mind and purpose. The written form of the promises becomes a promissory note—a written promise to fulfill the declared benefit.

One scholar says that Scripture contains more than thirty thousand promises related to the believer. But knowing the Bible holds thousands of promises is not enough. How do you, as a believer, take possession of those promises?

In a court of law, if you fail to fulfill a solemn pledge, such as a promissory note, you're guilty of breach of contract. Because of who God is, He can never be guilty of breach of contract. God cannot violate His promises. If He says something, then He must—by His very nature, which does not change— fulfill it.

Throughout the Bible God reveals Himself as the great promise-maker, and He keeps His word: "God is not a man, that He should lie, nor a son of man, that He should repent; has He said, and will He not do it? Or has He spoken, and will He not make it good?'' (Num. 23:19; see also 1 Kin. 8:56; Heb. 6:18-20; 10:23 and Is. 55:10-11).

Bounce-Back-Ability

The reflection of the divine character in creation is a glorious tribute to God's reliability. As God of the universe, He has all natural laws under His control, and nothing can stand in the way of the fulfillment of any promise He has made. He is omnipotent, and He never breaks a promise. If God has spoken something, it will happen—because God cannot lie.

As a pastor I often marvel at people who have a quality that I call ''bounce-back-ability.'' As I hear stories of despair and difficulty overcome in Christ, I see what God's grace can do. It's remarkable to witness what can happen to anyone who is willing to be rightly related to God through His Son, Jesus Christ.

As we move in faith, we learn that God's Word is reliable for every area of life. We can possess every promise that God has spoken if we will learn to reach out and claim what the Lord has given us.

Paul told the Galatians, ''But the Scripture has shut up all men under sin, that the promise by faith in Jesus Christ might be given to those who believe'' (Gal. 3:22). Paul affirmed that all, not some, of the promises of God have been fulfilled in Christ and are now available.

Taking Responsibility

Sometimes we're like the woman in 2 Kings 4:8-16. The prophet told her, "At this season next year you shall embrace a son" (v. 16).

Her response was disbelief: "No, my lord, O man of God, do not lie to your maidservant!" (v. 16).

Have you ever responded to a promise this way— especially when it was something you could hardly believe?

The Bible says you can prosper. The Bible says you can have peace of mind. The Bible says you can build a life that withstands storms. Don't respond with doubt. Say, "Yes, I *can* receive the things I need in life—not only for me, but for those around me as well."

One young woman in my church told me, "I was thirty-four years old before I knew I could rebuke Satan and trust God to remove the roadblocks hindering my life. The Christian life is more than attending church and having a quiet time of prayer every morning. I used to think that everything would be OK if I did only that. That was an innocent error. Now I know it's my responsibility to trust the word of the Lord in all things."

God's Checkbook

Charles Spurgeon, the great nineteenth-century English preacher, once said: "A promise of God may very instructively be compared to a check payable to order. It is given to the believer with the view of bestowing upon him some good thing. It is not meant that he should read it over comfortably and then be finished with it. No, he is to treat the promise as a reality—as a man treats a checkbook. He is to take the promise and endorse it with his own name by personally receiving it as true. He is by faith to accept it as his own."[2]

The promises of God are made out to *you*. Put your name on the blank line, then begin to persevere in faith and prayer.

All God's "promise checks" are dated in heaven, and with our finite knowledge we cannot know the time when they will be fulfilled. Many people become discouraged waiting for the fulfillment and end up doubting God, murmuring against Him and casting aside the promises.

God is never ahead of His time and never behind it. He always works on His timetable, not ours. We can see how that's true from Romans 4, which tells about Abraham pursuing the promises of God. Remember that God gave Abraham these precious promises when Abraham was eighty-six years old, but he didn't see the fulfillment of them until he was a hundred. For fourteen years he stood on the promises of God without wavering. Can you do the same?

Overcoming Unbelief

Romans 4 lists four factors that tell us how to possess the promises of God.

First, in verse 20 we see that Abraham did not "waver" or "stagger" in unbelief. Instead he "grew strong in faith, giving glory to God." The word *stagger* here means "to make use of one's own judgment and reasoning in discerning things." To stagger at the promise is to take into consideration the difficulties that lie in the way of seeing the promise fulfilled.

As you receive the promises of God, you too will have to deal with unbelief—with staggering. Sometimes the promise might seem absolutely impossible. How can this ever happen? you might ask. The only answer is that God said it would happen. Even when you see no natural way it can come about, you must still stand on the promise and refuse to stagger in unbelief.

When you doubt, you focus on your own power to accomplish. But that just magnifies the problem. Unbelief is strengthened when you focus on the natural, the physical, the temporal. Peter started out walking on the water. Then he took a closer look at the waves, doubted—and began to sink (see Matt. 14:30). Unbelief is the end result of focusing on your own power.

Growing in Faith

Second, Romans 4:20 says that Abraham "grew strong in faith." The more difficult the fulfillment, the more wonderful Abraham's faith. What a beautiful testimony of someone who was able to endure trials and grow in faith, instead of allowing unbelief to grow.

Faith is developed by learning from those in ages past whom God never let down or disappointed. Read the famous "faith chapter," Hebrews 11, and learn from the thirty-seven people listed there. God never disappointed them. They grew strong in faith and accomplished great things in God.

Strong faith produces desirable results. It honors God and judges Him as faithful to do what He has promised in our lives.

Full Assurance

Third, Abraham gave glory to God (Rom. 4:20). With the same kind of unquestioning confidence in all God's promises, you too can bring glory to God. It glorifies God when you trust in Him. You become a witness to His faithfulness and goodness when you proclaim His promises and your trust in Him.

Finally, Abraham was "fully assured that what He [God] had promised, He was able also to perform" (Rom. 4:21). In Isaiah 46:11 God tells us: "Truly I have spoken; truly I will bring it to pass. I have planned it, surely I will do it." He confirms that promise in Malachi 3:6: "I, the Lord, do not change." And Isaiah 40:8 assures us as well that "the Word of our God stands forever." What God has promised, He is able to bring to pass.

Abraham had full assurance regarding the promises of God. The Greek words we translate "full assurance'' actually provide a word picture of a ship carried forward under full sail, its canvas fully stretched out to catch the wind. Abraham had let out all his sails! He took a total risk to believe that God would do all that He said He would do.

Unlocking the Fortress of Doubt

Faith in God's promises is the key that unlocks the door of the fortress of doubt. Here are just a few of the thousands of promises you can unlock in your own life:

1. God's grace is sufficient. The mystery of inner strength lies in honestly encountering your own particular zones of weakness and powerlessness. The greater your inner ''deaths,'' the greater will be the outcome of God's supernatural grace in your day-to-day life.

God promises that His grace is sufficient for us in every situation (see 2 Cor. 12:7-9). One of God's Old Testament names was *El Shaddai*, meaning the almighty God, the all-sufficient one. We can't explain the all-sufficiency of grace. But as we pursue God, He becomes our strength, and His grace lifts us above all circumstances and causes us to be overcomers in Christ.

2. God's healing is available. In Exodus 15:26 God promises, ''I, the Lord, am your healer.'' (See also Ps. 103:1-3 and Matt. 12:15.)

The Bible proclaims repeatedly that God is our healer. Another Old Testament name for God was

Jehovah-Rophe, meaning "the God who is able to heal all our diseases at any time." Healing is available to all. It's true that at particular times God chooses to heal certain ones and not others. I don't understand that mystery. But we should always contend for healing, just as we contend in prayer for many things that we don't see with the natural eye.

The God Who Provides

3. God's supply is adequate. "And my God shall supply all your needs according to His riches in glory in Christ Jesus" (Phil. 4:19).

Yet another Old Testament name for God is *Jehovah-Jireh*, "the God who provides." This name is found in Genesis 22:9-14, where God provides the ram for Abraham to sacrifice in place of his son, Isaac.

This story provides us a great example of divine provision in time of need. And because you have the same God Abraham had, you can have the same provision in your time of need. You can stand on the promise that the Lord is your provider and that His provision is abundant. He is able to do exceedingly above all that you ask or think (see Eph. 3:20).

Keep this promise in mind as you pray for needs in your church, in your family and among your friends. Believe that God will provide miracle water and food for you whether you're in a spiritual wilderness like Elijah or in a time of physical need like Abraham. The Lord your God is your provider, and He will not fail you.

Romans 4 tells us to walk in the steps of Abraham's faith so that we might experience the same things Abraham did—the provision of God. If you have a need in your life right now, stop reading for a moment and pray, standing on this promise. Quote these Scripture verses aloud. Let your own ears hear the word of the Lord and build faith in your heart.

"I Am With You"

4. God's presence is sure. Surely the most radical revelation that has ever come to the human mind must be this: The God who created the vast universe would actually reach out to touch insignificant, self-centered, powerless people like you and me and share His life with us.

God promises in Genesis 28:15: "Behold, I am with you, and will keep you wherever you go, and will bring you back to this land; for I will not leave you until I have done what I have promised you."

You can apply this and other Scripture verses to your life right now:

> He has granted to us His precious and magnificent promises, in order that by them you might become partakers of the divine nature (2 Pet. 1:4).

> He Himself has said, "I will never desert you, nor will I ever forsake you" (Heb. 13:5).

> Lo, I am with you always, even to the end of the age (Matt. 28:20).

Surely you've experienced times of trial and distress. Times when you've felt that the presence of the Lord was no longer in your life. Times when you've felt rejected. But God's presence is sure! God says He will never reject you or leave you. He's always there, always available to you.

He Remains Faithful

5. God's faithfulness is reliable. Paul reminds us in 1 Corinthians 10:13: "No temptation has overtaken you but such as is common to man; and God is faithful, who will not allow you to be tempted beyond what you are able, but with the temptation will provide the way of escape also, that you may be able to endure it."

Lamentations 3:22-23 also promises us that God is faithful: "The Lord's lovingkindnesses indeed never cease, for His compassions never fail. They are new every morning; great is Thy faithfulness."

What a comfort! God's faithfulness will never fail you!

Even when we are unfaithful, God remains faithful. Even when we do wrong, God still does right. God's faithfulness endures forever.

These are just a few of the thousands of promises God has given us. I hope these will whet your appetite and spur you to dig into the Word yourself. As you do, write down the promises that apply to your own life. You'll be surprised how many pertain to you right now, no matter what situation you're in.

The promises of God are meant to be effective in your life, both materially and spiritually. But you must possess them by faith, prove them by obedience and inherit them through prayer. You can! Let your confession be, "Yes, I *can* possess God's promises!"

Yes,
I Can...

Be
Motivated!

otivation truly seems to be a mystery. Some have it; some don't. Without motivation you can't accomplish your God-given goals or fulfill your God-given potential for living. Without motivation you run carelessly and without enthusiasm. Motivation determines your strength, your commitment and your enthusiasm toward life.

Gas in the Tank

Motives are what drive us. The word *motive* means "a moving cause; an inner drive, impulse or intention that causes a person to do something or act in a certain way.'' As an old preacher once said, ''God made man to go by motives, and he will not go without them any more than a boat without steam or a balloon without gas.'' Motivation is to a Christian what gas is to a tank; it gives the energy needed to reach the destination.

Motivation can't be inherited. It's not passed from parent to child. It doesn't derive from family accomplishments. Nor is motivation environmental. It can't be passed on through friendship or acquaintance.

Motivation differs with each person. You may be highly motivated, while your brother or sister may have no motivation at all. Others may have ungodly motivations, driving forces such as self-gratification and pride that cause them to accomplish the wrong things. Yet others have yielded to the Holy Spirit and have godly motives to accomplish godly goals.

Biblical Models of Motivation

The Bible contains many examples of men and women who were motivated to accomplish their God-given goals.

■ God motivated Abraham by challenging him to trust in the vision that he—an old man—would become the father of many nations.

■ God-given dreams motivated Joseph, causing him to endure terrible trials, misunderstandings and disillusionment before the dreams ever came to pass.

■ The vision of the promised land motivated Joshua to fight for what was set before him.

■ Caleb was motivated by seemingly impossible odds to go where others refused to venture.

■ Jesus, too, was motivated by a clear purpose and destiny: "Jesus...for the joy set before Him endured the cross, despising the shame" (Heb. 12:2).

■ Paul was motivated by the prize of the upward call of God, by the knowledge that he had a mission to accomplish. "I count all things to be loss in view of the surpassing value of knowing Christ Jesus my Lord, for whom I have suffered the loss of all things, and count them but rubbish in order that I may gain Christ" (Phil. 3:8).

■ Timothy was motivated by the apostolic influence of his spiritual father, Paul, and by an understanding of what it meant to live in the light of eternity.

Danger Signs

How is your motivation? Is it not what it used to be? Not what it ought to be? Paul Meyer, an authority on self-improvement through personal motivation, lists five danger signals of diminished motivation:

1. Doubt. Questioning your ability to do the job. Self-confidence is lost; worry and confusion take over.

2. Procrastination. Putting off important decisions, hesitating to take risks, hoping the problem will take care of itself.

3. Devotion to false symbols. Surrendering to egotism and status seeking; coveting the job title instead of concentrating on better ways to do the job; desiring to be well-thought-of instead of legitimately productive.

4. Complacency. Surrendering to the inner urge that almost everyone has to "take it easy"; being satisfied with "good enough" instead of "excellent."

5. Loss of purpose. Failing to make concrete plans for going anywhere else. Reaching the initial goal becomes the end of the career, instead of another beginning.[3]

If you're thinking, That's me you're talking about! then this chapter is for you. Yes, you *can* become motivated. Yes, you *can* accomplish great things in your life. But you must understand what motivation is from a Christian standpoint, discover that motivation and release it in your own life.

As God Sees Us

If money, location, health or anything else were not an obstacle, what would you do with your life right now? What would you like to have written on your tombstone as the final testimony to your life?

Before you answer, remember that godly motivation is seeing yourself the way *God* sees you and the way the Bible says you can be. Motivation is linked to a number of different factors:

1. Character. Motivation always flows from what you value. What you value most will become your priority. If you have a true born-again experience with Jesus Christ, understand the power of the Holy Spirit and are being shaped into the image of Christ, then your motivation will flow out of the new creation you are. On the other hand, if you're overcome by fleshly habits and carnal reasoning, then your motivation level will be linked to that kind of character.

2. Dreams. Paul says in Philippians 3:13-14: ''I do not regard myself as having laid hold of it yet; but one thing I do: forgetting what lies behind and reaching forward to what lies ahead, I press on toward the goal for the prize of the upward call of God in Christ Jesus.'' Paul had definite dreams and goals that motivated him to live an energetic life.

It's important to strike a balance between dreams and reality. Be realistic about your limitations. Attempting the impossible will destroy your motivation overnight. Stretching is one thing, but suicide is another!

Ask yourself, Am I overextending? Have I set goals that are too high? You need to accomplish *some* things to motivate you to accomplish *great* things. Begin today by motivating yourself with goals you can reach this week and this month. Then you can extend them to one-year, five-year and lifetime goals.

A God Without Limit

3. Calling. Every motivated person in Scripture understood that they had a destiny. They were called by God for a specific reason. You too have been called to accomplish certain things in your life. You have a God-given task, a God-given place—a spot no one else can fill. Like a bird that finds its nest, so is a person who finds his or her calling.

4. Sensitivity to the Holy Spirit. The Holy Spirit is the motivating force behind the whole universe. As you stay in constant fellowship with Him, He'll motivate you. As your prayer life increases and you learn to recognize the voice of the Holy Spirit, He'll build motivation into your total person.

5. Understanding of God's Word. When you study God's Word, you come to understand who God is, how big He is and what He can do. You learn to trust in a big God—a God without limit. You believe that nothing is impossible with God!

The Word has life in it. As you keep it, confess it and rejoice in it, it will become life to you. As you memorize and meditate on Scripture, it will change your thinking habits and become a motivating factor in your life.

Invest in Eternity

6. Fear of God. Proverbs 1:7 says, "The fear of the Lord is the beginning of knowledge." Do you know that you're accountable for every word, thought and action of your life? You're living your life before the Lord. So live every day keeping in mind your investment in eternity. God has given you the air you breathe, the body you inhabit and the mind you think with. Don't waste your life doing your own thing—you belong to Him! Someday we'll all stand before the judgment seat and answer for everything we do. Contemplate the judgments and rewards of God. Now that's motivating!

7. Spiritual gifting. If you're called to be a teacher in the body of Christ, then you're probably motivated to study more than someone who's called to be an exhorter or who has the gift of healing and miracles. When you discover your spiritual gift, you give your life to that particular area. As you do, your motivation grows.

For example, if you feel God is calling you to be a missionary to Japan, you'll be highly motivated to learn Japanese. You wouldn't have the same motivation to learn Spanish or German.

Similarly, if you feel called to serve, you'll keep your eyes open for opportunities to serve. You'll be available when tables are set up or taken down or when the kitchen staff needs help. You'll be there when the nursery coordinator asks for help. You may not have wanted to serve before you became a Christian. But once you discover your spiritual gift, it becomes a powerful motivating factor in your life.

Refilling the Tank

8. Risk-taking. Imagine Joshua's challenge: Moses was dead, and now Joshua had to take Israel across the Jordan and into the promised land. Three times the Lord told him to be strong and courageous (see Josh. 1:6,7,9).

As it was for Joshua, your motivation is linked to your ability to rise to challenging experiences. If you fear the task set before you, your motivation will be squelched. Don't be afraid of new ideas, new methods or new surroundings. Willingness to take risks can be a motivating factor in your life.

9. Reservoirs. Just as you can't run a car with an empty fuel tank, you can't run your life with an empty spiritual fuel tank. Ephesians 5:18 says, "Be filled with the Spirit." That's the premium-grade fuel you need to run on. You also need to store up energy, hope, ideas, spiritual power and vision. You'll fill up on them by spending time in prayer, Bible study, even relaxation.

Maybe you've been involved in a job or ministry that has drained you of your energy, ideas and spiritual power. You've lost the cutting edge of your vision, and you're growing discouraged. Now is the time to step aside and fill your reservoir once again with the spiritual elements that will motivate you to reach your goals.

If you're running on empty, it's possible to motivate yourself for a while through sheer willpower. But sooner or later you'll suffer burnout. If you're thinking, That's me, make plans to spend more time by yourself, more time with your wife and family, more time away from your busy job, and more time with the Lord.

Mental Junk Food?

10. Right thinking. "Whatever is true, whatever is honorable, whatever is right, whatever is pure, whatever is lovely, whatever is of good repute, if there is any excellence and if anything worthy of praise, let your mind dwell on these things" (Phil. 4:8).

A recent survey showed that 52 percent of Americans go to a psychologist or psychiatrist or end up in a mental health clinic. Why? Because their thinking is wrong! What you think will become a habit, and your habits will form your character, and your character will determine your destiny.

Tell me your thoughts, and I'll tell you your destiny! Be careful what you let into your mind. If you feed your mind junk food, what do you think will happen to your motivation? It will wither and eventually die. But if you meditate on the Word and read other material that nourishes your thinking, your motivation will grow.

11. Commitment to follow the Lord. We read in Joshua chapter 14 the inspiring story of Caleb—a great achiever, thinker and man of God. Caleb did not shrink back from challenges. His secret of achievement, even at an old age, was that he wholly followed the Lord. Caleb was not frustrated in midlife. He had clear moral standards and goals, because he knew he was committed to God.

Motivation is not just a state of mind; it's also a state of heart. As your commitment to Jesus Christ grows, so will your motivation. A commitment to follow the Lord without reservation is a vital step to releasing the kind of motivation that will keep you for a lifetime.

Enlarging Your Heart

12. Prayer. Prayer truly is essential to long-lasting motivation. It deepens your commitment to God's purposes and allows you to remove obstacles to that commitment on a daily basis. Romans 8:26 says, "And in the same way the Spirit also helps our weakness; for we do not know how to pray as we should, but the Spirit Himself intercedes for us with groanings too deep for words."

This verse speaks about praying by the Spirit. Sometimes it's difficult to know what to pray, but the Holy Spirit has the mind of God continually. As you give yourself in prayer to the Holy Spirit, you'll enlarge your heart, which in turn will enlarge your capacity to be motivated. Prayer releases you from stress, wrong thinking, bad attitudes, sin, unrighteousness and anything else that can rob you of motivation. A praying person is a motivated person.

The Portrait of Faith

13. Faith. Did you know that you can be disloyal to God by making small what He intended to make large? Look at the heroes of Scripture listed in Hebrews 11. Faith motivated each of them to go beyond the normal and against the impossible. Faith motivates when the flesh gives out. When the natural man stops, faith goes forward and motivates from within.

A pastor wanted to encourage an aspiring young artist who was a member of his church. He handed him a check for five hundred dollars and said, "Paint me a picture depicting your interpretation of faith."

Several months later the artist unveiled his painting: a strong, warm and happy portrait of Jesus Christ. When the pastor asked why he chose Jesus as his subject, the artist replied, "Galatians 2:20 says that I have been crucified with Christ and I no longer live, but Christ lives in me. The life I live in the body, I live by the faith of Jesus Christ. Well, if He gives the faith, then He should be the perfect picture of faith!"

Faith allows you to see the invisible and hear the inaudible. It allows you to take the kingdom of God and make it reality. As your faith grows, your motivation will grow.

Reaching Higher

14. Attitude. None of the other factors listed here can improve your motivation if you don't have the right attitude. Successful people are motivated by an optimistic attitude—an attitude of "Yes, it can be done"; "Yes, I can do this"; "Yes, the Lord is for me"; "Yes, the Bible works"; "Yes, I can be motivated!"

You can reach higher and further than you ever thought possible—when you have the right attitude.

A person with the right attitude will get a job done when others are still wringing their hands and explaining why it's impossible!

Optimists inspire themselves to action. They believe in who they are and what they're doing. They make mistakes and learn from them. Optimists know that with God's help they can be the people they were created to be.

The Ultimate Freedom

It takes work, but it *is* possible to change a bad attitude. Victor Frankl discovered through his experiences in Nazi concentration camps that "the last of the human freedoms [is] to choose one's attitude."[4] If you've suffered from a tendency to negative attitudes, you don't have to stay that way. Second Corinthians 5:17 says, "If any man is in Christ, he is a new creature; the old things passed away; behold, new things have come." Whatever your past may have done to you, you can make a fresh start.

You can develop a brand-new attitude within your heart and spirit. You can get up every morning with a happy spirit, starting your day with a positive confession: "It's another good day for me. I expect something good to happen to me today, and I expect God to answer my prayers. I know the Lord will direct me today!" These are the confessions of someone who is molding a positive attitude.

Start Today!

If you lack motivation, stop right now and pray. Ask the Holy Spirit to restore your motivation. Maybe you were motivated once, but something has happened to you, and you're not so sure of your goals anymore. Something has caused you to become lukewarm and discouraged.

You can restore your motivation starting today. Read over the fourteen factors listed in this chapter and honestly evaluate where you stand on each one. Ask the Lord to help you in areas where you're lacking.

Then read some inspirational materials and autobiographies. Learn about William Carey, David Livingstone, Paul Yonggi Cho and other men and women who have accomplished great things. Fill your mind with the principles demonstrated in their lives.

Next ask God to readjust your perspective on life. Look at life through God's eyes and through the eyes of the Bible.

New Mountains to Climb

Maybe you've already accomplished what you set out to do, and you have no more challenges. Find a new challenge. It might take a job change, more education or a different ministry outreach. Look for new mountains to climb.

By the way, don't discount the importance of good health. If your body is out of shape, chances are your motivation is too. When your body functions improperly, fatigue sets in, and your body works against your spirit, causing you to lose your motivation.

Finally, whatever happens, don't be satisfied with mediocrity. Look at motivation as a form of exercise. Thinking about exercise will not improve your circulation. Get up and run! The secret of motivation is to take that all-important first step and do what God expects of you.

Yes, you *can* be motivated!

Yes,
I Can...

Have a
Living Faith!

he word *faith* in its various forms is used 558 times in the New Testament. By contrast, the word *love* is mentioned 258 times; righteousness, 230 times; and hope, 85 times. Based on these statistics alone, we can conclude that faith is a primary subject of the Bible.

Have you ever asked yourself, How can I have a living faith—a real faith—a faith that equips me for living in the twentieth century?

The Bible speaks about "the faith," meaning the body of revealed truth on which we stake our lives. Scripture also refers to "saving faith" by which we enter into a relationship with God and maintain our position in Christ. But the type of faith we'll study in this chapter is "living faith," that everyday faith by which we can live and maintain the power of Christ in our lives.

The Fruit of Faith

Living faith isn't merely intellectual assent to a creed; it's tied to action. The letter of James reminds us that faith can be dead if it doesn't display certain vital signs of action (see James 2:17). He isn't writing here about saving faith, but about the appropriate conduct that should flow out of living faith. True faith is like a tree: It will reveal its life by the fruit it produces. James proclaims loudly and clearly that we must examine our faith to see whether it may be dead (see James 2:14).

Dead Faith

What are some characteristics of dead faith?

1. Dead faith is merely head faith. Intellectual assent by itself is tragically inadequate. James points out that demons also believe and shudder (see James 2:19). You can believe a promise yet fail to exercise faith to appropriate it. But living faith is spiritual and heartfelt.

2. Dead faith is merely tongue faith. It's words without action. James says that genuine faith can't see a brother or sister in need and respond simply,

"Go in peace, be warmed and filled." Living faith must be more than words.

3. Dead faith makes God's Word of no effect. Jesus chastised the Pharisees for "invalidating the word of God" by their "tradition" (Mark 7:13). One great sin of modern humanity is its tendency to nullify the Word of God in favor of our merely human traditions. Dead faith has a way of making the Word of God useless through its religiosity.

If you identify with any of these characteristics, you need to ask the Lord, How can I change my dead faith to a living faith? It's so easy to drift from a living faith to a dead one, from zeal to lukewarmness. Paul wrote, "Test yourselves to see if you are in the faith; examine yourselves! Or do you not recognize this about yourselves, that Jesus Christ is in you—unless indeed you fail the test?" (2 Cor. 13:5).

Living Faith

What are some signs of a living faith?

■ **Living faith speaks with the mouth what is in the heart.**

Romans 10:8 says, " 'The word is near you, in your mouth and in your heart'—that is, the word of faith which we are preaching." When you received Jesus Christ into your heart, you did it by confessing with your mouth. Your mouth was instrumental from the very beginning of your Christian walk in activating the living faith that God imparted to you.

The apostle Paul was a verbal torch. He had a living

faith that surged outward in his speech, touching everyone nearby with its virtue. Jesus' words had a similar effect; Luke tells us that those around him "were amazed at His teaching, for His message was with authority" (Luke 4:32). The disciples also confessed their faith with their mouths; Acts 4:31 says they "began to speak the word of God with boldness." To change your dead, lukewarm faith into a living faith, start by using your mouth. Confess what the Bible says about you, about your circumstances and about your God. Speak words that will build your spirit up, not tear it down.

■ **Living faith comes by hearing the Word of God.**

In Luke 1:38 Mary responded to God's messenger by saying, "Be it done to me according to your word." Acts 17:11 says that those who heard the gospel at Berea "received the word with great eagerness." In Colossians 3:16 Paul exhorts us, "Let the word of Christ richly dwell within you."

Living faith is fed by the living Word. As you feed on the living Word, the power of the living Spirit will move through your living heart and produce living actions. Your faith comes alive!

■ **Living faith activates spiritual gifts.**

It gives you the power to declare the person you are becoming and to chart your course toward a magnificent destiny.

When you know that you possess what the Bible *says* you possess, you can build faith to *activate* what you possess. When you activate your gift with your living faith, you allow God to make your life count for Him.

Many people wait around for their spiritual gifts to activate themselves, then wonder why the Lord doesn't use them. The Holy Spirit wants to use you right now. But you must activate your gift through a living faith, governed by your prayer and your response to the Word of God.

■ **Living faith stands strong.**

It never quits in the face of adversity. Paul tells us in 1 Corinthians 16:13, "Be on the alert, stand firm in the faith, act like men, be strong." When you have a living faith, you're not moved by circumstances or pressures. You can stand in the face of adversity. Living faith changes a moody Christian into a stable man or woman of God who is able to resist the devil and stand firm.

■ **Living faith is evidenced by a disciplined life-style.**

This cultivates godly character. Second Peter 1:5 says, "Applying all diligence, in your faith supply moral excellence." Make every effort to supplement your faith with godly character, "applying all diligence" to character development as the Scripture commands. All of us need moral excellence coupled with our living faith.

■ **Living faith obeys the Word of God.**

This applies even when God's Word seems to be in conflict with the natural mind. We see this in the account of Peter and the disciples in Luke 5. Although they had been fishing all night and had caught nothing,

Jesus told them to let down their nets on the other side of the boat.

Peter's mind questioned the Lord's command. But his response is classic: "Master, we worked hard all night and caught nothing, but at Your bidding I will let down the nets" (v. 5). In other words, "I don't get it, but I'll do it just because You have asked me to." He obeyed and netted such an enormous catch of fish that the nets broke.

God wants you to receive blessing, enlargement and increase. But you must let down your nets of faith to take up the great catch God has for your life. That takes obedience.

■ **Living faith moves in the power of the Holy Spirit.**

Living faith obeys the Scripture when it says to worship with uplifted hands, clapping, shouting and singing to God. Dead faith says this is foolishness. But living faith sees this as a way to lift up Christ in victory and to obey the Scripture.

■ **Living faith prays.**

It recognizes prayer as the way to see God move in human affairs. Prayer in faith sees God moving, working and doing the impossible. But the carnal mind sees prayer as a waste of time, because dead faith sees prayer as unreasonable.

■ **Living faith sees giving as a way of increase.**

Tithing is foolish to the natural man. Give away 10 percent of your income and live on only 90 percent? That's foolish to anyone who doesn't believe the Bible. But the Bible says that if you scatter you'll increase, while if you hold back you may lose what you already have.

■ **Living faith honors baptism.**

It sees baptism as a way to identify with Christ's death and to receive circumcision of the heart. Even though the event is invisible, it's real.

■ **Living faith sees speaking in tongues as a way to release the Holy Spirit.**

To the natural mind, speaking in a spiritual language sounds childish, embarrassing and ridiculous. Yet the Bible says it edifies us as we communicate supernatural things to God (see Jude 20).

■ **Living faith moves us to become committed to a local church.**

God wants you in a local expression of His family, serving with your time, energy and talents, taking responsibility for people, discipling and teaching. As you do, you may encounter burdens and even abuse from other believers. But you'll also have the opportunity to pray with others, do spiritual warfare, recharge your spiritual batteries and be fed.

■ **Living faith will be tested.**

I know a man who once shared his heart's desire for a strong, unshakable faith. He told me how he prayed whenever he looked at brick or stone walls: "Lord, make me stronger than that wall!"

Soon he noticed he had more than his share of trouble, with one problem after another coming into his life. Finally, in exasperation, he sought the Lord and discovered these obstacles were part of God's plan to answer his prayer. Faith grew as he asked the Lord for wisdom and vigor to attack his problems.

Stretching Our Faith

We must exercise our faith if it is to be effective. Like a muscle, faith grows by stretching. If we desire our faith to be strengthened, we shouldn't shrink from the times our faith is tried.

Remember Abraham. He refused to allow a questioning mind to undercut his faith. He refused to be ruled by fears about the future. Instead he was ruled and governed by the kingdom of God and the supernatural leading of the Holy Spirit. Romans 4:20-21 says he "did not waver in unbelief, but grew strong in faith, giving glory to God, and being fully assured that what He had promised, He was able also to perform."

Through the prophet Isaiah God announces, "I have planned it, surely I will do it" (46:11). Through Malachi He declares, "I, the Lord, do not change" (3:6). Isaiah sums up God's promise this way: "The word of our God stands forever" (Is. 40:8).

What God has promised, He is able to bring to pass. Abraham had full assurance regarding the promises of God. Living faith honors God by counting Him able and being fully persuaded of God's willingness and ability to keep His word.

By God's grace, yes, you *can* have a living faith!

Yes,
I Can...

Be a
Rejoicing
Christian!

verybody is searching for happiness, but few find it. True, some have found a super-ficial kind of happiness. But that is only temporary. It doesn't satisfy the inner person.

The world's definition of happiness is self-gratification—pursuing new thrills and new excite-ment. This kind of hedonism seeks out lust, passion and pleasure for their own sake. If pleasure be-comes central to your life, it soon dominates your life. You become worn out trying to feed its un-controlled cravings. Eventually you become enslaved to it.

A Pleasure-Crazy Society

Titus 3:3 describes people who are enslaved to this world's value system:

> For we also once were foolish ourselves, disobedient, deceived, enslaved to various lusts and pleasures, spending our life in malice and envy, hateful, hating one another.

These are people who live for the moment. They forget the importance of long-range goals. They take advantage of others to meet their own selfish desires. A life like this, lived solely for selfish pleasure, is a life doomed to sorrow.

Sadly enough, we live in a society that has gone pleasure-crazy. For many, pleasure is the highest priority in life. Paul foresaw this situation when he wrote that the people who live in the last days will be "lovers of pleasure rather than lovers of God" (2 Tim. 3:4). Thus his warning holds true today: "She who gives herself to wanton pleasure is dead even while she lives" (1 Tim. 5:6).

Proverbs 21:17 adds to that insight: "He who loves pleasure will become a poor man." And Jesus referred to this type of person when He said, "They are choked with worries and riches and pleasures of this life" (Luke 8:14). Despite their pursuit of pleasure, their true inner condition is miserable: "Even in laughter the heart may be in pain, and the end of joy may be grief" (Prov. 14:13).

Filling the Inner Void

When you lose something important, you search for it. If you can't find it, you may try to replace it with some substitute, hoping to find satisfaction. This is true of people who lack inner peace. They search high and low for something to fill the void inside them. To some people this leads to a continual change of places to live, friends, jobs, recreation, churches, religions, health kicks, dress, and so on.

The search for genuine inner joy is never-ending—when you conduct it apart from the reality of Christ. When you look for fulfillment in people, places, positions or possessions, joy becomes illusive.

■ You can't control people—where they live, how they treat you or how many friends you have.

■ You can't control places. They eventually bore you, or you get transferred to a job in another place.

■ You can't control possessions. A single fire can destroy everything you own.

■ You can't control positions. Others can take them away from you, as can an unstable economy. You can never climb high enough to have total security.

Your security can *only* be in Christ, in His kingdom and in the eternal realities His Word promises you.

True Joy

In the lyrics of his famous hymn "A Mighty Fortress Is Our God," the great Reformation leader Martin Luther said:

Were they to take our house,
  Goods, honor, child, or spouse,
Though life be wrenched away,
  They cannot win the day.
The Kingdom's ours forever.

True joy is established in the eternal realities of Christ and His kingdom. Although biblical joy has an emotional component, it must be based soundly on a clear understanding of a right relationship to God. No superficial stimuli can serve as an adequate substitute for the deep foundations of genuine joy.

True Christian joy has its roots deep in God. Circumstances, moods, seasons, people or possessions do not affect this kind of joy. According to Romans 14:17, "The kingdom of God is not eating and drinking; but righteousness and peace and joy in the Holy Spirit."

Foundations of Joy

Four foundation stones must be in place if we are to live in the joy of the Lord.

■ **The first foundation stone is turning to God with all your heart so that you trust in Him for all your life.**

Paul wrote to the Romans: "May the God of hope fill you with all joy and peace in believing, that you may abound in hope by the power of the Holy Spirit" (15:13). This means responding to the gospel and God's plan of forgiveness, cleansing and acceptance through the blood of Jesus. Turning your life over to God and trusting in His plan are essential to permanent joy.

■ **The second foundation stone is entering into kingdom living.**

This means more than salvation. It includes coming under the government of God, His ways and His laws. It involves making Jesus Lord of every area of your life—actions, thoughts, even hopes and dreams. God is the king; you and I are His servants.

■ **The third foundation stone is love for righteousness that affects the way you live.**

Righteousness means right actions, right attitudes and right convictions.

The Bible talks about two types of righteousness: *positional* righteousness and *practical* righteousness. By right relationship through faith in Jesus we obtain a right standing, not by works or by law (practical righteousness), but by trusting in Christ (positional righteousness). Practical righteousness is the behavior that results from right relationship to Christ. When your righteousness is off kilter, your peace and joy will be too.

The writer of Hebrews reveals the pattern for entering into the joy of the Lord: "Thou hast loved righteousness and hated lawlessness; therefore God, thy God, hath anointed thee with the oil of gladness above thy companions" (1:9). The Lord Jesus Christ loved righteousness and hated iniquity; consequently, He was anointed with the oil of joy.

You and I must love what is right and hate what

is wrong as Jesus did. We must love justice and hate lawlessness. When we become a friend to what is right and an enemy to what is wrong, we're able to enter into the joy of the Lord.

■ The fourth foundation stone is the Holy Spirit.

Joy isn't found in the flesh, in the world, in circumstances or in people. True joy can only be found in the Holy Spirit.

God has called us to be joyful and to reflect that joy to the world. When you're crowned with the joy of the Lord, circumstances and the "Monday blues" can never diminish that joy or take it away from you. But if your source of joy is something other than Christ, you'll always be disappointed.

Enjoy God

What do rejoicing people look like? Let me give you several signs:

1. Rejoicing people worship with joy. The psalmist says: "Thou wilt make known to me the path of life; in thy presence is fulness of joy; in thy right hand there are pleasures forever" (Ps. 16:11). The Lord wants to make you full of gladness. At His right hand are delights that will endure forever, an unbounded joy He'll reveal to you as you stay in His presence. Why waste time on the temporary pleasures of the world when the Father has in His right hand everlasting pleasures that can satisfy your inner man eternally?

2. Rejoicing people enjoy God. It is reported that an atheist philosopher once remarked that Christians would have to look more redeemed if they expected him to believe in their Redeemer.

Take a good look in the mirror. Do you see a bored person? Are you always whining about the heavy dealings of God and the hard times you're so bravely enduring? Or do you have your nose so buried in the Scriptures that nobody can understand what you say?

God wants you to enjoy His presence: "Let all who take refuge in Thee be glad, let them ever sing for joy; and mayest Thou shelter them, that those who love Thy name may exult in Thee" (Ps. 5:11).

Parents, do you realize the Bible says that, if you don't serve the Lord with joy, your children will go into bondage, and you'll lose them to the world? (See Deut. 28:41.) How many young people do you know who hate church and God because they live with parents who never rejoice in the Lord? If Bible reading, church attendance and Sunday school are trials to be endured for the parents, it's no wonder their children never want to set foot in a church.

As adults the greatest thing we can do for our young people is to enjoy God—to laugh, have fellowship, enjoy one another, enjoy worship and enjoy everything that has to do with the kingdom of God.

3. Rejoicing people know how to laugh. When you listen to joy, you usually hear laughter, just as sorrow usually manifests itself in crying.

The Psalms express great joy: "Then our mouth

was filled with laughter, and our tongue with joyful shouting; then they said among the nations, 'The Lord has done great things for them' '' (126:2). "How blessed are the people who know the joyful sound!" (89:15). Laughter is the sound of flowing joy. If you've lost your laughter, your relationship with the Lord may be suffering.

Joy in the Midst of Trouble

4. Rejoicing people rejoice *in spite of* circumstances, not *because of* circumstances. In 2 Corinthians 7:4 Paul says, "I am overflowing with joy in all our affliction." Even in the midst of many troubles, your cup can be full of consolation and overflow with true biblical joy. Paul wrote to the Philippians that he had learned to be content in all circumstances (see Phil. 4:11). When he and Silas were chained in prison, their backs bleeding from the beatings they had received, they could still sing praises to God, because their joy wasn't based on circumstances.

Paul tells us in 1 Thessalonians to give thanks in *all* situations and circumstances (5:18) and "rejoice in the Lord *always*" (Phil. 4:4, emphasis added). Rejoice when everything goes wrong. Rejoice when nothing pleases you. Rejoice when you face disillusionment and disappointment. The key to living a successful Christian life is true biblical joy.

The prophet Habakkuk outlines the attitude of a mature Christian living in the joy of God:

Though the fig tree should not blossom,
And there be no fruit on the vines,
Though the yield of the olive should fail,
And the fields produce no food,
Though the flock should be cut off from the
  fold,
And there be no cattle in the stalls,
Yet I will exult in the Lord,
I will rejoice in the God of my salvation.
The Lord God is my strength,
And He has made my feet like hinds' feet,
And makes me walk on my high places
  (3:17-19).

You might be facing some rather grim circumstances. Maybe you've lost your job. Maybe your cupboards and refrigerator are looking mighty empty—not to mention your bank account. Perhaps your child or spouse has been sick. That's when you need to rejoice in the Lord most and put your trust in Him. He is your strength.

Health and Strength

5. Rejoicing people have good health. "A joyful heart is good medicine, but a broken spirit dries up the bones" (Prov. 17:22). A rejoicing heart does the body good. Joy works an excellent cure and makes for a quick recovery.

According to Dr. Ern Crocker of Sydney, Australia, people who find it easy to laugh have fewer heart attacks. If laughter could be ordered at the corner drugstore, doctors would prescribe many laughs a day.

6. Rejoicing people are strong in the Lord. Nehemiah told his people not to mourn or weep, but rather to rejoice, "for the joy of the Lord is your strength" (8:10).

Biblical joy, properly tempered with continual dependence on the help of God, is a powerful means of strengthening the soul. When you're filled with joy, every duty is delightful.

Hope in the Midst of Sorrow

7. Rejoicing people weep with hope of the morning. Out of his own experience the psalmist declares, "Weeping may last for the night, but a shout of joy comes in the morning" (30:5). As a Christian you're not immune to trials and disappointments. Life will sometimes throw you a curve—a death in the family, the debilitating illness of a loved one, disappointment by a close friend or church member. When that happens, sorrow can quickly fill your heart, a true sorrow that you can't ignore or confess away.

The Bible says rejoicing people *can* weep. But they weep with hope. The hope is that morning will come. This trial will pass. This sorrow of heart will soon go away and rejoicing will return once again.

One of the pivotal leaders in my church is our worship leader, Jim Eschenbacher. Jim is a lean, tall, good-looking guy who has spent most of his life building houses, raising a family and singing.

Jim has known what it is to weep in the night and find joy in the morning. Several years ago Jim's wife was treated for a common cold in her physician's office. She had a sudden negative reaction to the medication and died. Needless to say, the shock and sorrow were extremely difficult for Jim to bear as he took on the role of both father and mother to three little children.

After a period of time Jim wrote a song to the Lord in memory of his beloved wife. He decided to arrange a session to record cassette tapes for use in his ministry. One of the young women he hired as a background singer is now Jim's wife. Jim knew weeping— but joy came right behind.

Joy and Obedience

8. Rejoicing people rejoice as an act of their will. To rejoice as an act of the will is to rejoice by bringing your will into godly submission to the will of God—by bringing your soul into obedience to the Word of God. It is moving from emotionalism to obedience. It is taking the moods of the flesh and bringing them under the rule of God.

Two words that appear over and over in the Psalms are "I will": "I will give thanks to the Lord with all my heart; I will tell of all Thy wonders. I will be glad and exult in Thee; I will sing praise to Thy name, O Most High" (9:1-2). "My heart shall rejoice in Thy salvation. I will sing to the Lord'' (13:5-6). ''I will rejoice and be glad'' (31:7). ''I will bless the Lord at all times'' (34:1). Do you see how discipline brings about true continual joy? It's not an outcome of your emotions; it's an act of your will.

Right now confess that, yes, you *can* be a rejoicing Christian. Yes, you *can* control your moods by disciplining your will. Start by saying, ''I *will* rejoice in this situation. I *will* give thanks to God at all times.'' You'll be surprised, as I have been at times—for when your will takes the lead, everything else follows.

9. Rejoicing people love faith challenges. Jesus endured the cross for ''the joy set before Him'' (Heb. 12:2). What faith challenges are set before you today? The cross you have to bear may be heavy. But *for the joy that is set before you*, you can endure any pain and climb any mountain that God puts before you. Faith can be a joyful experience when it has its roots in God.

Yes, you *can* be a rejoicing Christian!

Yes,
I Can...

Be a
Harvester!

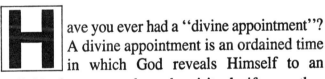ave you ever had a "divine appointment"? A divine appointment is an ordained time in which God reveals Himself to an individual or group through spiritual gifts or other spiritual phenomena. God arranges these encounters to demonstrate His kingdom.

John 4:28-38 tells about Jesus' encounter with a Samaritan woman. While she was drawing water from a well, He told her about spiritual water that would be much more valuable to her. On that day the woman had a divine appointment with Jesus.

The Model Harvester

Jesus is the model harvester. He was continually winning people to the kingdom of God—at least twenty-seven conversions are recorded in the four Gospels, including:

- Andrew (John 1:40-41);
- Peter (John 1:41-42);
- Philip (John 1:43-45);
- Nathanael (John 1:45-51);
- Nicodemus (John 3:1-21);
- a Samaritan woman (John 4:29);
- a nobleman (John 4:53);
- the adulterous woman (John 8:11);
- a blind man (John 9:38);
- Martha (John 11:27);
- a centurion (Matt. 8:5-13);
- Matthew (Matt. 9:9);
- a Canaanite woman (Matt. 15:28);
- a demoniac from Gadarene (Mark 5:15-20);
- a woman with internal bleeding (Mark 5:28-34);
- a Galilean leper (Matt. 8:2);
- the father of a demonic boy (Mark 9:24);
- Bartimaeus (Mark 10:46-52);
- a paralytic in Capernaum (Luke 5:20);
- a sinful woman (Luke 7:38-50);
- a Samaritan leper (Luke 17:18-19);
- a tax-gatherer (Luke 18:13);
- Zaccheus (Luke 19:8-9);
- an infirm woman (Luke 13:11-13);

■ Mary Magdalene (Mark 16:9);
■ a centurion (Matt. 27:54);
■ a dying thief (Luke 23:42).

One by One

Throughout the Gospels Jesus reaped the harvest person by person, miracle by miracle, encounter by encounter. He wasn't just winning the multitudes to the kingdom of God. He was winning people one by one.

The great strategy of reaping the harvest in this day and age is to see the multitudes as individuals and to ask for a supernatural divine appointment with them to lead them into the knowledge of the Lord. Jesus wants to bring people across your path and into your life so that you can touch them with His Spirit.

I remember a divine appointment that happened to two couples I know. The husbands, Craig and Richard, had just returned from a three-day retreat. As they entered Craig's home, Craig's wife, Marcia, introduced them to a friend of hers. During the small talk that followed, they learned she was on her way to her first sky-diving lesson. Craig and Richard talked with her about this high-risk adventure and then shared the even greater adventure she could experience in accepting Jesus Christ as her Savior.

Without any convincing arguments or efforts at persuasion this young woman immediately turned her life over to the Lord. "This is what I've been searching for all my life!" she said. With a calm, quiet joy in her heart she prayed. She was awed at the presence of God who lovingly captured her heart. What a great example of the lengths to which Jesus will go to introduce people to His kingdom!

Get Rid of "If"

Do you, too, hunger to be a harvester? To have divine appointments? To minister to people's needs with the same spiritual sensitivity Jesus had? You *can* be a harvester! The first step is to confess, "Yes, I *can* help reap the harvest in these days. Yes, I *can* be a prayer warrior. Yes, I *can* move in the Holy Spirit. Yes, I *can* believe for miracles."

Perhaps you're skeptical. Perhaps you think you need more training, more anointing or more time. Get rid of the "if" mentality. "*If* I get trained...*if* God opens a door...*if* I feel bold...*if* the harvest begins to ripen...*then* I'll move in with my sickle."

Into the Fields

As I write this chapter, it's late summer here in Oregon. The countryside is filled with fields of ripened grain and orchards of heavily laden fruit trees. Roadside produce markets are ready for a booming business. Everywhere I look I see the harvest waiting to be reaped. But it doesn't happen with only one or two people doing all the work. Everyone pitches in to bring in the harvest.

Similarly, the spiritual harvest will never be reaped

by apostles, prophets, evangelists, pastors and teachers only. The five ministries referred to in Ephesians 4:11-12 are not to do all the reaping of the harvest. Rather they're to *train* the rest of us so that *we* might become harvesters.

We may be tempted to look to the church or the pastor to do all the work. But think about all the unsaved people you come in contact with day in and day out. God has put you and them together in a divinely appointed meeting so that you, not your pastor, can touch them with the gospel of the Lord Jesus Christ.

A Call to Action

Many seminars today teach evangelism. Many conferences train evangelists. Many churches hold preaching series and teaching classes on how to be fishers: how to "bait the hook," how to "reel them in." We don't have a lack of knowledge; we have a lack of *action*. Consider the following parable:

Now it came to pass that a certain group called themselves fishers. And lo, there were many fish in the waters all around. In fact, the whole area was covered with streams and lakes filled with fish. And the fish were hungry.

Week after week, month after month, year after year, these people who called themselves fishers met in meetings and talked about their call to go fishing. Continually they searched for new and better methods of fishing and for new and better definitions of fishing. They sponsored congresses to hear about new fishing equipment. They built large, beautiful, fishing headquarters. The only thing they didn't do was fish!

All the fishers seemed to agree that what was needed was a board to challenge fishers to be faithful in fishing. The board was formed by those who had great vision and courage to speak about fishing, to define fishing and to promote the idea of fishing in faraway streams and lakes where many other fish of different colors lived. Elaborate training centers were built so they could teach fishers how to fish.

The Futility of "Fishology"

Those who taught had doctorates in fishology. But the teachers did not fish. They only taught about fishing. Some spent much time learning the history of fishing and traveled to faraway places where the founding fathers had gone fishing in centuries past. They lauded the faithful fishers of yesteryear who handed down the idea of fishing.

Many of the fishers sacrificed much and put up with all kinds of difficulties. They lived near the water and bore the smell of dead fish every day. They endured the ridicule of people who made fun of their fisher clubs. They anguished over those who were not committed enough to attend the weekly fishing meetings. After all, were they not following the Master who said, "Follow Me, and I will make you fishers of men"?

Imagine how hurt some were when one day a person suggested that those who didn't catch fish were really not fishers, no matter how much they claimed to be. Yet it did sound correct. Is a person who never catches a fish really a fisher?

A Great Harvest

Pat Robertson, host of "The 700 Club" television show, has stated, "This is the time for the harvest of the nations. The greatest revival is yet to be seen, and churches will never hold the increase unless they start thinking in the thousands."

South African evangelist Reinhard Bonnke began with a meeting tent that held ten thousand people. Today he has a tent that seats thirty-four thousand. He calls this the age of the "combine harvester."

In the Gospels Jesus speaks about the harvest in several places. In Matthew 9 He tells His disciples, "The harvest is plentiful, but the workers are few. Therefore beseech the Lord of the harvest to send out workers into His harvest" (v. 37-38).

In the parable of the wheat and the tares (Matt. 13:24-31) and the parable of the seed (Mark 4:26-29), Jesus says there will be a great harvest both now and at the end of the age. He encourages His followers to reap a great harvest daily.

"Look on the Fields"

Harvesting is the work of every Christian. You must, of course, move in the Holy Spirit and in power evangelism in order to accomplish this great task. And you must know your exact place in the harvest—whether you are a sower, a waterer or a reaper. But no matter what your profession or ministry, you're called to help reap the harvest.

How do you become a harvester? Jesus says, "Look on the fields, that they are white for harvest" (John 4:35). The Greek word for *look* means "study with intensity."

God told Abraham: "Now lift up your eyes and look from the place where you are...for all the land which you see, I will give it to you and to your descendants forever...Arise, walk about the land through its length and breadth; for I will give it to you" (Gen. 13:14-17). You, too, must arise and walk about the harvest land, lifting up your eyes to see all that God has for you.

The Lord told Moses: "Lift up your eyes to the west and north and south and east, and see it with your eyes" (Deut. 3:27). And he told the nation of Israel through the prophet Isaiah: "I will bring your offspring from the east, and gather you from the west. I will say to the north, 'Give them up!' and to the south, 'Do not hold them back' " (43:5-6). These promises are ours as we reap the harvest.

The Harvest Prayer

In our church we pray a harvest prayer, turning in each direction—north, south, east and west—saying, "Give them up; hold not back! Release them and let them go." We believe that the spiritual powers holding people in bondage must obey our command. We lift up our eyes to the north and to the south, to the east and to the west, believing that the harvest will be released.

Several other Scripture verses also give us hope for the harvest:

> Lift up your eyes and look around; all of them gather together, they come to you....You shall surely put on all of them as jewels, and bind them on as a bride (Is. 49:18).

> Lift up your eyes round about, and see; they all gather together, they come to you. Your sons will come from afar, and your daughters will be carried in the arms (Is. 60:4).

> Lift up your eyes and see those coming from the north. Where is the flock that was given you, your beautiful sheep? (Jer. 13:20).

> Let your eyes be on the field which they reap, and go after them (Ruth 2:9).

As a harvester you should pray, "Lord, allow me to see the harvest round about. Allow me to see those that are ready to be reaped."

Ask God for a genuine spiritual burden for those who are unsaved. Carry this burden in your prayers and with a sincere concern manifested in your actions toward the unsaved.

Never Give Up

Harvesting may require hours of sweat, toil and endurance in bearing the cross as you're led to love the unlovable. God may put someone on your heart who's angry, insensitive, intolerant and verbally abusive. Loving this person into the kingdom may be a demanding challenge that tests your patience.

Think of harvesting as a job complete with a job description that you will live by. Prepare yourself to be a laborer who knows your job, your message and your God. This takes work. It doesn't come automatically by sitting in the pew during church services. Learn the gospel message, gospel Scripture passages, gospel stories. Learn how to lead someone in a prayer to receive Jesus Christ. Learn how to answer the hard questions. Learn more about God's nature so you can introduce Him to someone who doesn't understand what He's really like.

Never give up on anyone. Persevere in reaping the harvest even when it seems impossible. Love without human reasoning, with tolerance toward those who practice pagan life-styles. If you become critical of their life-style, you'll become self-righteous and condemn them in their sin.

Live out your Christian life with joy, thereby showing those who are unbelieving that being a Christian doesn't mean you can't have fun.

Begin to think of those people whom the Lord has put into your life. You *can* be a reaper of the harvest!

Overcoming Obstacles

In a casual survey conducted at the church I pastor, we found that people become members of a church in several ways:

■ Six to 8 percent just walked in on their own.

■ Two to 3 percent came through a church program they had heard about.

■ Eight to 12 percent were attracted by the pastor's ministry.

■ Three to 4 percent came because of a special need.

■ One to 2 percent were invited by church members through outreach.

■ An overwhelming *70 to 80* percent were invited by relatives and friends who already had a relationship with them.

What obstacles keep you from reaching out to your friends and relatives, to those people you meet each day through "divine appointments"? If you'll change your attitude right now, the Holy Spirit will strengthen you in His Word.

Confess to yourself and those around you, "Yes, I *can* be a harvester. Yes, I *can* reap the harvest that the Lord has put into my life. Yes, I *can* reap the harvest represented by my friends, my relatives and all those I'm involved with.''

As you take on a new attitude, the Holy Spirit will lead the way and open doors you could never open by yourself. Remember, the harvest is ripe and ready. God is able to save anyone. And you are called to do His work and His will: bringing the gospel of Jesus Christ to those around you right now.

Yes, you *can* be a harvester!

Yes,
I Can...

Be a
Godly
Father!

EIGHT

Martin Luther once said, "I have difficulty praying the Lord's Prayer because whenever I say, 'Our Father,' I think of my own father who was hard, unyielding and relentless. I cannot help but think of God that way." Children tend to form their view of God according to how they feel about their own fathers.

To build strong churches and a strong society we must have strong families. The foundation of society has always been the family unit. Today we face a society that is degenerating, and the collapsing family unit is definitely part of the problem.

Today more than ever we need godly men. We have weak churches today, because we have weak families. We have weak families, because we have weak husbands, weak fathers and weak men. This chapter addresses the role of fatherhood in today's society and how we can develop godly fathers who will raise up a godly generation.

[A note to the reader: Perhaps you're a single mother. You find yourself living out the roles of both mother and father. Through my pastoral counseling experience I know something of your struggles and the demands life makes upon you. As you read these pages, please capture the spirit of what I'm saying to the godly father. I'm speaking to you as well.]

The Dandelion Factor

Did you know that the official flower of Father's Day is the dandelion? The dandelion was chosen, it's said, because the dandelion, when trampled upon, grows better. I hope the Dandelion Factor is true, because the role of the father has certainly been trampled on in our day.

The breakup of the family unit is at an all-time high. More and more homes have both parents working and latch-key children. The traditional roles of parents are undergoing drastic changes, even to the point of discussing legislation to allow homosexuals to become adoptive parents. Identity problems and new family pressures surface continually. Television portrays Dad as a wimp and Mom as a boss.

As James Dobson writes in *Parenting Isn't for Cowards*, parenting "is demanding but parents in the twentieth century have saddled themselves with unnecessary guilt, fear and self-doubt...This [raising children] can be a happy, hopeful and successful experience."[5]

The Godly Father

No magic formula can make you the godly father God wants you to be, but I can offer you some guidelines to follow. All of them flow from Scripture. We can't rely on our own experience, our own natural father's example or television to show us the model father. Only God can tell us what a father is to be, because God the Father is the greatest model in the universe. And His Word illuminates His principles. Here to guide you are twelve scriptural characteristics of a godly father:

1. A godly father is born again. "Unless one is born again, he cannot see the kingdom of God" (John 3:3).

Spiritual rebirth occurs when you believe in your heart and confess with your mouth that Jesus Christ is your personal Lord and Savior. If you've truly been born again, you'll have a change of heart, mind and life-style. You'll have a new love for your wife and children. You'll function differently from the way you did before.

I don't mean becoming religious and legalistic. Attending church, giving money and helping the Boy

Scouts doesn't make you a Christian, and it won't make you a godly father, either! If you already feel like a failure as a father, remember that when you were born again you became a new creation; old things passed away, and all things became new (see 2 Cor. 5:17). You can rid yourself of negative images, negative models and negative ideas of fatherhood, replacing them with a scriptural idea of fatherhood that you can live out through the power of the Lord Jesus Christ.

Build on the Bible

2. A godly father respects and obeys God's Word. "How can a young man keep his way pure?" the psalmist asks. "By keeping it according to Thy word" (Ps. 119:9).

To be a godly father you need to love the Word of God and make it central to your life and home. I don't mean just displaying a big family Bible on the coffee table. I mean living out the Word of God in a fashion that causes your wife and children to hunger after God. The Bible must be your final authority for all decisions, including those concerning the children.

Have you ever told jokes that belittled the Bible or its standards? Have you ever ridiculed Christian leaders for taking the Bible too literally? Have you ever said that the Bible is not applicable to the problems of our day? Have you ever justified questionable activity by claiming that the Bible can be interpreted different ways? Have you ever brought into your home books, magazines or videos that blaspheme the standards of God's Word? Have you ever encouraged your wife or children to do things that were contrary to the standards of the Bible?

If you're guilty of any of these, go to God in prayer. Ask Him to forgive you and to restore your love and respect for the Bible.

Set aside time for family devotions. Choose Scripture verses that the entire family can memorize. Make a commitment that nothing will come in the way of these family times. Remember, if your children don't learn respect for God's Word at home, they won't learn it at church or in Sunday school.

Clean Hands, Pure Heart

3. A godly father rejects the impurities of our day. ''He who sows iniquity will reap vanity, and the rod of his fury will perish'' (Prov. 22:8). To sow iniquity means to sow moral impurity. Impurity destroys the work of the Holy Spirit, because the Holy Spirit is sent from a holy God, and He cannot work in the midst of sin. He can only work in a heart where impurities do not dwell.

Impurity destroys your love for God and for God's family. It destroys your ability to discipline effectively. Impurity in a particular area will cause you to be indulgent in that area with your own children.

Impurity can also destroy your sensitivity to the needs of your family. If you want to be a godly father, you must not allow impure thoughts or habits to rule your life. Guard what you see, what you read, what you say, how you think and what you let into your mind.

Pornography is an extremely harmful weapon of the enemy. It destroys a man's love for God, his wife and his children. It damages a man's marriage through mental adultery and distorts a man's view of love, binding him with a spirit of lust.

If you want to raise your family in the ways of God, treat pornography as you would treat a poisonous snake that's ready to strike you. Most likely you're exposed to some sort of pornography every day: posters on the job, billboards on the freeway, ads in magazines, commercials on television. Avoid those things you can avoid; simply remove them from your presence. And don't allow your mind to dwell on those things you cannot avoid.

Standing Guard

4. A godly father fears the Lord. Fear of the Lord flows from awareness that you are in the presence of a holy, just and almighty God—that every thought, word and deed are open before Him and are being judged by Him. ''By the fear of the Lord one keeps away from evil'' (Prov. 16:6). ''The reward of humility and the fear of the Lord are riches, honor and life'' (Prov. 22:4).

5. A godly father is alert to destructive influences that could damage his home and family. Think about the influences your children and wife are exposed to every day—influences that shape the way they think, act and feel, such as television, music and secular education.

How much do you know about what's going on in the schools today? Do you read the books your children bring home? What are they learning about God, morals, philosophy for living? Are they learning that abortion is right? That homosexuality is an acceptable "alternative life-style"? That churches are bigoted and narrow-minded and make people feel guilty? That things are "different" today because we live in a "new era" where people have the right to live any way they want?

Read Psalm 101:2-7 and Deuteronomy 7:6, then make sure that no ungodly things enter your home: pornographic books or magazines, sensual materials; objects related to horoscopes, fortune telling, ouija boards; music that rebels against authority or moral standards; books by false religions or cults; rebellious or immoral friends.

Instead, fill your house with good Christian music and books, Bibles, devotional guides and biographies of great men and women of God. Adorn your walls with statements of your submission to God and of His greatness and beauty.

At All Times, Love

6. A godly father loves each child by recognizing individual worth and potential. As a godly father you must recognize strong points and weak points in each member of your family. Emphasize the strong points and see how you can provide training that will strengthen the weak points.

A father loves at all times, whether a child is wrong or right. Children may break your heart by doing evil, but you must never make them feel that you will disown them. Discipline your children, but never let them feel that you love them any less because you have to discipline them.

Partiality is one of the great hindrances to true love flowing in the family. If you are constantly partial to one child, your other children will rebel—not only against you, but also against the favored sibling. Don't allow partiality to dwell in your home.

7. A godly father cultivates good manners. Love must be demonstrated in actions. Your manners demonstrate to others what you really think about them, so poor manners are clear evidence that you don't respect your wife and children or cherish them as important people. A father's poor manners will infect the entire family. Your sons will develop disrespect for their mother and their sisters. Your wife and daughters will develop aloofness toward men.

Good manners are often more important to women and children than they are to men. Your family has probably already mentioned things they'd like for you to change, things that embarrass them. So listen to them and cultivate good manners out of respect for them.

A Worker Who Serves the Lord

8. A godly father provides for his family through a balanced work life. A godly father doesn't let his family live in need. Paul told Timothy, "If anyone does not provide for his own, and especially for those of his household, he has denied the faith, and is worse than an unbeliever" (1 Tim. 5:8).

We need to rid ourselves of a wrong attitude about work. Genesis 3:17-19 reveals that God created humankind to work by the sweat of our brows. We are to till the ground and labor for what we receive.

Significantly, throughout Scripture the giants of faith had strong ties to what we call "secular work." They tended sheep, built cities, wrote music, served kings, practiced medicine, caught fish, collected taxes and taught school—all while serving God. The call to business is just as legitimate and godly as any other call. Work itself is a calling.

Two common extremes in our society are wrong: Some people despise work, and others worship it. Do you consider work as a necessary evil and define the ideal job as one that pays a lot for doing little? That's a wrong attitude that God will not bless. Or do you worship your work as though it were a god, bending your knee before the altar of your career? That's idolatry. God isn't pleased with that attitude, either, and won't bless it.

Don't despise your work, and don't worship it. You need to be a faithful and wise worker, serving God while also building your family. If work is taking all your time so that you neglect your family, you need to change your work schedule and habits.

Taking the Pulse

9. A godly father monitors the spiritual health of his children. Where do your children stand spiritually? Church attendance doesn't tell the whole story. I was raised in church, and I know how easy it was in my youth to fake interest and put on a spiritual "front." All the while I was backslidden and on my way to hell!

Look for clues to where your children are spiritually:

■ Listen to what they like to talk about. Kids will talk about what they really love and are interested in.

■ How do they respond when you bring up spiritual matters? Do they constantly question you about your own standards and ideas for living? Do they call it "your" choice?

■ What kind of people do your children choose as friends?

■ Be alert to early stages of rebellion. The Bible says that "rebellion is as the sin of divination [witchcraft]" (1 Sam. 15:23). If your children are showing signs of rebellion, explain to them what it is and what it will do to their lives.

Husband, Love Your Wife

10. A godly father loves his children's mother. A child needs to know that Mom and Dad love each other and will stay together. Some children who have never seen their fathers showing affection toward their mothers develop a wrong view of women. Children need to see affection between their parents, because they catch more from what they see than from what they're taught in books. If you love your wife with all your heart and treat her with respect, your children will experience greater security.

If you and your wife do have problems, don't discuss them in front of your children. This will only undermine their sense of security. If you feel a blow-up coming, don't vent it in front of the children; go to a private place to resolve your differences. If your family or marriage has unresolved tension, seek Christian counseling.

Good marriages are probably one of the greatest needs in America. Teenagers especially need to see that marriages can last, that divorce is not the way out, and that the covenant made in marriage, "Till death do us part," can be lived out in spite of a culture that actively seeks to destroy marriages.

The Model Father

11. A godly father is a godly model. Providing a godly model for your children influences them more effectively than teaching and preaching. Whether you like it or not, you're on stage before an audience that's watching your every move.

Are you telling them one thing but doing another? Do you tell them the best things in life are free but fill your temporal castle with expensive toys and status symbols? Do you teach your kids to be kind and considerate while you habitually shout obscenities at careless drivers? Do you preach honesty and respect for the law but cheat on your income taxes and install a radar detector in your car? Do you speak out against drugs and alcohol and then use them yourself?

What do you show your children about your priorities? Do you put your work ahead of them? What do they learn about morality from watching you—and from watching what you watch on television?

How about faith? Do you teach them to trust in God? Or to trust in themselves? Or in money?

It's Never Too Late

12. A godly father never quits. God offers hope. James Dobson once wrote an article entitled ''It's Never Too Late to Change.'' In the article he includes a prayer for every father who has ever felt he has failed:

> Lord, you know my inadequacies. You know my weakness, not only in parenting, but in every area of my life. I did the best I could, but it wasn't good enough. As You broke the fishes and the loaves to feed the five thousand, now take my meager effort and use it to bless my family. Make up for the things I did wrong. Satisfy the needs that I have not satisfied. Wrap Your great arms around my

children and draw them close to You. Be there when they stand at the great crossroads between right and wrong. All I can give is my best; and I've done that. Therefore, I submit to You my children and myself and the job I did as a parent; the outcome now belongs to You.[6]

Many parents feel defeated every day. I understand the emotions that go with parenting—those times of anger when the entire day has gone wrong and little Johnny finishes it off by spilling the milk or knocking over a plant. Maybe you've lost your temper. You've said things you shouldn't have said. You aren't a perfect human being, and you're not a perfect parent.

Perhaps you're in the midst of a divorce. Maybe you were raised in a broken home yourself.

Whatever your situation, you *can* be a godly father. You can take the points in this chapter and put them to work in your own life. Write them down on index cards and pray about them daily. Over a twelve-day period, write down your own thoughts on each of these points, being honest about how you can improve.

Yes, you *can* be a godly father through the power of our risen Savior, the Lord Jesus Christ. You cannot do it on your own—He won't let you! Christ is here to help you—*now*. Stretch out your hands to the heavenly Father. Ask Him to give you the strength to be the father He wants you to be.

Yes,
I Can...

Keep on
Keepin' On!

he biblical Greek word for *perseverance*, *hypomone*, is used thirty-two times in the New Testament. Sometimes translated "patience," "endurance" or "patient waiting," the term literally means "remaining under" or standing firm despite opposition.

In life you will undoubtedly face many battles. At times you'll think other people have it easier than you do—and you may well be right! But the Bible says joy is based not on an absence of difficulty but on unearthing your gifts and employing them for the benefit of the kingdom. With God's grace empowering you, you can do all things in Christ.

This is why the Bible puts so much emphasis on the quality of perseverance, the ability to "keep on keepin' on." As Winston Churchill so aptly put it, "Persistence is what gives losers a winner's edge. Persistence is what makes winners out of losers, what makes winners out of quitters."

Heroes of Perseverance

Thomas Edison didn't give up when he failed in his first efforts to find an effective filament for the incandescent lamp. He did countless experiments with hundreds of different kinds of materials. As each failed, he would toss it out the window. The pile eventually reached the second story of his house! But he didn't give up. He sent men to China, Japan, South America, Jamaica and Burma in search of fibers and grasses to be tested in his laboratory.

One weary October day in 1879—after thirteen months of repeated failures—Edison picked up a bit of lamp black, mixed it with tar and rolled it into a thin thread. The thought occurred to him to try a carbonized cotton fiber. For five hours he worked, but the thread kept breaking before he could remove it from the mold. He used up two spools of thread before a perfect strand emerged at last—only to be ruined as he tried to place it in the glass tube.

Edison still refused to admit defeat. He continued without sleep for two days and nights. Finally he managed to slip one of the carbonized threads into a vacuum-sealed bulb. He turned on the current and at last saw what he had so long desired to see.

He Never Gave Up

Edison conducted some eighteen thousand experiments before he achieved his goal. Many others during his lifetime were performing some of the same experiments. But one difference between Edison and the others was that Edison never gave up. His persistence gave the world the electric light bulb.

Edison is only one example of heroic perseverance. Dr. Jonas Salk worked three long years, with many failures, before he finally succeeded in developing a vaccine for polio. Abraham Lincoln failed in six attempts at political office before he was elected president. I understand that Albert Einstein, often considered the greatest genius of the twentieth century, once said, ''I think and think for months, sometimes for years. Ninety-nine times the conclusion is false, but the hundredth time I am right.''

The Power of Encouragement

While exercising at a health club recently, I observed a group of weight lifters cheering a comrade on as he strained to pump a heavy load of iron. ''You can do it! Go for it!'' they yelled. And he did it.

The thought struck me: I doubt that he would have been able to lift all that iron if they had shouted, ''Forget it! It's too heavy! You can't do it. You'll hurt yourself.'' The power of encouragement is the lifeblood of success.

I want to encourage you today, wherever you are as you read this book—in the kitchen, on a bus, on an airplane, sitting in a classroom or at a park—to consider what a difference perseverance can make in your life.

Threats to Perseverance

What causes perseverance to decay? In Hebrews 12:1-17 the writer lists nine threats to perseverance:

Threat number 1: Unconquered sins.

This threat is described in verses 1 through 3. Verse 1 stresses "lay[ing] aside every encumbrance, and the sin which so easily entangles us." What sins— even the little sins that cling so closely—are hindering you?

The extra body weight an athlete sheds during training is not sin, but it's still worth getting rid of. Ancient Greek runners raced practically naked, with every weight discarded, so that they might run the race without any encumbrances.

Similarly, some things that aren't wrong in themselves can still hinder you from putting forth your best effort. These are the unconquered, insignificant areas of your life that undermine your perseverance; for example, carnal moods of selfishness or even recreation taken to an ungodly extreme.

Threat number 2: Undefined goals and purposes.

Verse 1 in this chapter exhorts us: "Let us run with

endurance the race that is set before us.'' The long-distance runner must have a goal, a mark to hit. How close are you to reaching your goal? More important, at what are you aiming?

''Serendipity'' means experiencing those wonderful ''chance happenings'' that everyone loves to encounter. Many people trust their futures to these hopeful ''chance happenings'' and by doing so constantly surrender the satisfaction and fulfillment God would give them if they were committed to some clear goals for their lives.

We all need short-range, along-the-way milestones to evaluate our progress in life. Undefined goals and purposes will cause us to become frustrated and live a life without challenge.

The Bible outlines certain goals we should shoot for:

■ Becoming like Jesus Christ in character and life-style.

■ Developing the fruit of the Spirit and seeking out the gifts of the Spirit.

■ Living a life that glorifies God in everything we do.

■ Working and providing for our families.

■ Being a good wife, husband or child.

■ Maintaining a godly character in an ungodly society.

It's impossible to hit these marks without setting concrete intermediate goals against which to measure our progress.

Threat number 3: Deadly distractions.

According to verse 2 we are to fix our eyes on

Jesus, the author and perfecter of our faith, because He is the only true model for everything we are to become. We are to have eyes for no one and nothing else.

"Fixing" your eyes means more than just a casual glance. It refers to a disciplined, intent gaze. You must not allow anything to turn you aside from the goals and visions God has given you.

In Philippians 3:14 Paul says, "I press on toward the goal." By keeping his eye single, Paul was able to avoid distractions, endure trials and accomplish what God set out for him to do.

What deadly distractions are diverting your eyes from the perfect mark God has for your life? What deadly distractions has Satan put in your path? Is it the love of pleasure, the cares of life, overindulgence, deceitfulness of riches, double-mindedness, lust, moral breakdown, murmuring, bitterness, resentment, laziness? What area of weakness has Satan targeted in your life?

Threat number 4: Losing motivation.

The writer of Hebrews says that Jesus "for the joy set before Him endured the cross" (v. 2). Motivate yourself by continually reviewing the reason you began. The Lord Jesus was able to endure the cross, because He knew what the cross would accomplish. He was able to see beyond the suffering by keeping His eyes on the reward. He knew that His death, burial and resurrection would deal a mortal blow to Satan's stronghold.

Christ could see beyond the cross to the church

victorious, the army of God rising in all the earth. He could see beyond the cross to His second coming to reign with ten thousands of his saints forever. He could see beyond the cross to the time when He would be seated at the right hand of the Father, making intercession for the saints as the high priest of our profession.

You too must look beyond your suffering, even beyond your own life. You must see how your life will affect your children, your grandchildren and your great-grandchildren. You must see how your decisions today will affect others. Looking beyond your own circumstances is a key to perseverance.

Threat number 5: Becoming weary.

"Consider Him who has endured such hostility by sinners against Himself, so that you may not grow weary and lose heart" (Heb. 12:3).

How tough are you on yourself? Are you a firm taskmaster? Are you making hard decisions or soft decisions about your schedule, the commitments you're trying to keep, the goals you intend to reach?

Someone has said, "When God opens a door of opportunity, it's a sin not to walk through it." The more you say yes to these opportunities, the greater the pressures will be to wear you down. Weariness and discouragement can quickly set in and threaten your perseverance.

The Greek word for *weary* is *kamno*. It relates to long-distance runners and how they can experience the gradual letting down of effort and the relaxing of discipline after reaching a goal.

Look at Gideon. God gave him the strength to defeat the Midianites, but after his victory he relaxed his moral virtue and inner strength. Because of his laxity all Israel began worshipping an idol. A great victory became a great defeat, because he became weary in doing what was right (see Judges 8).

Look at Solomon. He built the temple and saw the glory of God descend upon it. But after the work was finished he relaxed, and his strength and creativity turned into lust, greed and wrong decision-making (see 1 Kin. 11).

Be careful not to grow weary in doing what is right. Pay particular attention after great victories or in times of stress, strain and challenge. It's often right after the greatest victories that Satan will attack most cunningly.

Threat number 6: Wrong focus.

According to verse 4 of this chapter, "You have not yet resisted to the point of shedding blood in your striving against sin."

If you focus on your hardships, they'll soon become greater than they really are. Don't allow self-pity to rule your spirit and pervert your perspective. Instead pursue your endeavors with a realistic appraisal of the difficulties to be expected. In Romans 8:18 we read that the present sufferings are not worth comparing to the glory that shall be revealed.

Therefore we do not lose heart, but though our outer man is decaying, yet our inner man is being renewed day by day. For momentary, light affliction is producing for us an eternal weight of glory far beyond all comparison, while we look not at the things which are seen, but at the things which are not seen; for the things which are seen are temporal, but the things which are not seen are eternal (2 Cor. 4:16-18).

Keep your focus on the things of God. Don't allow your mind to focus on hardships, or molehills will become great mountains in your path.

Threat number 7: Reacting against God's discipline.

God does not discipline His people aimlessly but with a definite end in view. You can endure hardship and discipline, if you can understand that God is treating you as His very own son or daughter.

And you have forgotten the exhortation which is addressed to you as sons,

"My son, do not regard lightly the discipline of the Lord, nor faint when you are reproved by Him; for those whom the Lord loves He disciplines, and He scourges every son whom He receives."

It is for discipline that you endure; God deals with you as with sons; for what son is there whom his father does not discipline? But if you are without discipline, of which all have become partakers, then you are illegitimate children and not sons.

Furthermore, we had earthly fathers to discipline us, and we respected them; shall we not much rather be subject to the Father of spirits, and live? For they disciplined us for a short time as seemed best to them, but He disciplines us for our good, that we may share His holiness.

All discipline for the moment seems not to be joyful, but sorrowful; yet to those who have been trained by it, afterwards it yields the peaceful fruit of righteousness. Therefore, strengthen the hands that are weak and the knees that are feeble, and make straight paths for your feet, so that the limb which is lame may not be put out of joint, but rather be healed (Heb. 12:5-13).

The purpose of discipline is not to destroy you or discourage you but to produce something good in you. You will become stronger, not weaker, because of God's discipline. But when you react against God's correction, you're reacting against the very tool that will shape and mold you and give you strength for living.

Threat number 8: Discouragement.

"Strengthen the hands that are weak and the knees that are feeble, and make straight paths for your feet, so that the limb which is lame may not be put out of joint, but rather be healed'' (vv. 12,13). We must avoid the temptation to grow discouraged. As the biblical proverb reminds us, ''If you are slack in the day of distress, your strength is limited'' (Prov. 24:10). Paul confirms that truth when he tells the Galatians they will reap if they ''do not grow weary'' (6:9).

Discouragement develops progressively according to a typical pattern. First comes frustration, then depression, vain imaginations, criticism, resentment, bitterness and finally unbelief. By that time your heart is drained of energy. You can't function in your spiritual ministry. You suffer the paralysis of discouragement.

Sometimes you can be like a dead car battery: You need to be jump-started back to life. If you feel like that dead battery, look to God as your battery charger. He'll come to bring you consolation, strength and encouragement. He'll come alongside you to lift you up.

If discouragement is threatening your perseverance, you can shake it off today and look to God for encouragement that will cause you to succeed instead of fail.

Threat number 9: Bitterness.

The writer of Hebrews cautions us: ''See to it that no one comes short of the grace of God; that no root of bitterness springing up causes trouble, and by it many be defiled; that there be no immoral or godless person like Esau, who sold his own birthright for a single meal'' (12:15-16).

This scriptural passage echoes Deuteronomy 29:18, which says, "Lest there shall be among you a root bearing poisonous fruit and wormwood." When you have a root of bitterness in your life, you bear poisonous fruit that's as bitter as wormwood. The fruit may be slow in manifesting itself, but when it appears it will be bitter.

Bitterness defiles us. It makes us unfit to stand before God. When allowed to grow, bitterness contaminates everyone who comes in contact with it.

Stand Your Ground

Work at developing perseverance in your life. The threats listed in this chapter give you an idea of what you're up against. To overcome these obstacles, make commitments to a goal in times of pressure, and don't give up either in time of war or in time of peace. Unite yourself to those of like mind. They'll help you withstand destructive influences. Put aside any privileges or "nice things" that weaken your stand or your strength.

In 2 Samuel 23:11-12 we find the account of a man named Shammah, who stood in the midst of a little hill of beans he had planted. When the enemy tried to take it from him, he stood his ground and brought a great victory for his family and his people. He fought so long, in fact, that his fingers became glued to the sword. They couldn't pry them off—he was so intent on winning! Shammah had the spirit of determination and perseverance. He never gave up.

The apostle Paul never gave up, despite ship-wrecks, beatings and disloyalty from friends and churches alike (see 2 Tim. 4:7). He fought the good fight. He finished the course. What a testimony from this old warrior, who was able to write about all his trials and yet say, "I never gave up." You can say the same thing.

Yes, you *can* keep on keepin' on!

Yes,
I Can...

Live Out
My Dreams!

ave you ever watched a professional golfer standing in a sand trap with sweat streaming into his eyes, preparing to make his shot? What is he thinking? What picture does he see in his mind? He sees one thing—the ball in the hole! If he didn't have a dream, he'd never see it happen.

The future belongs to those who have dreams. Those who have dreams and the faith to live them out truly live lives of excitement and fulfillment.

What are your dreams? God wants to help you fulfill them! He wants to make your purpose in life become a reality, and He will help you develop to your fullest potential. He has a definite life plan for you, and He'll help you accomplish it.

Paul wrote to the Ephesians: "Therefore be careful how you walk, not as unwise men, but as wise, making the most of your time, because the days are evil. So then do not be foolish, but understand what the will of the Lord is" (5:15-17).

What do you believe God has for your life? What do you think He wants your function to be in the body of Christ? What are your private dreams and hopes? How can they become realities? What would you attempt in life, if you knew it was impossible to fail?

Dreams and Visions

God begins every miracle with a seed picture—the invisible idea that gives birth to a visible blessing. Your dreams and desires begin as photographs within your heart and mind. God plants these pictures in you as invisible seeds and then waters and nurtures them into reality.

Paul Yonggi Cho, pastor of Yoido Full Gospel Church in Seoul, South Korea—the largest church in the world—says that dreams and visions are the language of the Holy Spirit. The Holy Spirit may be speaking to you right now about your life. Shouldn't you be listening carefully?

"Would that all the Lord's people were prophets," Moses said, "that the Lord would put His Spirit upon them!" (Num. 11:29). In the New Testament that prayer is answered on the day of Pentecost when Peter quotes Joel: " 'And it shall be in the last days,' God says, 'that I will pour forth of My Spirit upon all mankind; and your sons and your daughters shall prophesy, and your young men shall see visions, and your old men shall dream dreams' " (Acts 2:17). One aspect of such prophecy is God's speaking to individuals about their future.

As God pours out His Holy Spirit, both at the time of your salvation and as you continue to walk in the Spirit, He sends the spirit of prophecy so that you can have insight into your future to understand what God wants to do with your life. This insight creates a bright vision, raises your motivation level and supplies a mighty stimulus to work hard for fulfillment.

To dream means to anticipate what is to come to pass and to contemplate it with pleasure. To dream is to have a fond hope, an aspiration for the future, an expectation for something good. To dream is to be totally overtaken by desire that motivates you toward your destiny. To dream is to face every obstacle with the determination of a winner.

Setting a Course

When God gives a dream, He also gives a specific course in life to fulfill. Paul said, "But I do not consider my life of any account as dear to myself, in order that I may finish my course, and the ministry which I received from the Lord Jesus, to testify solemnly of the gospel of the grace of God" (Acts 20:24). Paul had a course that charted his life.

Five elements must be in place in your life for you to fulfill your course and accomplish your God-given dreams.

1. You must find your course in life. Romans 8:28-30 gives the plan for doing this:

> And we know that God causes all things to work together for good to those who love God, to those who are called according to His purpose. For whom He foreknew, He also predestined to become conformed to the image of His Son, that He might be the first-born among many brethren; and whom He pre-destined, these He also called; and whom He called, these He also justified; and whom He justified, these He also glorified.

Here Paul introduces what might be called the "technical terms" of his theology.

■ **You have been** *foreknown.* This means "known beforehand by God, but not yet made manifest to us." God's foreknowledge is the basis of His foreordaining counsel for your life.

■ **You are** *predestined.* God knows beforehand the particular boundaries and limitations He has put into your life. Predestination is always based on fore-knowledge. God has marked you, because He knows the end from the beginning, and He has predetermined certain aspects of your life—your parents, your nationality, the way you look, your habits and personality.

■ **You have been** *justified.* That is, you have been

legally and formally acquitted from guilt and pronounced righteous. Therefore, you don't have to deal with guilt and condemnation as you try to fulfill your dreams, even if you stumble in the process. When you understand this position, you can rest in Christ and not frustrate yourself by trying to become something you're not.

■ **You are** *called.* The Greek word here means to "embrace an invitation by the Spirit of God for some specific task." Someone once said that a calling is a purpose in life so enjoyable that we're eager to do it regardless of the reward or compensation. Thomas Edison reportedly said, "I never worked a day in my life. It was all play."

Finding your course in life involves understanding foreknowledge, predestination, justification and calling, and then applying them in a practical manner. Meditate upon these words. Think about the specific purpose God has called you to. Can you write down that purpose? Can you state your dream concretely? Consider spending some time in prayer and fasting to determine God's course for your life.

Count the Cost

2. You must count the cost before launching out. Jesus said, "For which one of you, when he wants to build a tower, does not first sit down and calculate the cost, to see if he has enough to complete it? Otherwise, when he has laid a foundation, and is not able to finish, all who observe it begin to ridicule him" (Luke 14:28-29).

Have you counted the cost of the dream God has given you? Do you understand that God's call for you won't be without testing and trials and sometimes even sorrow? Understand that when you launch out to fulfill your dream you'll encounter challenges far above your own strength that can be fulfilled only in the strength of God.

Joseph was a dreamer, though he had no idea of the cost of his dream (see Gen. 37). He had a great future, yet it was with great consequence and great price. His brothers hated him and were full of jealousy and envy. Even his own father didn't understand his dream.

During Joseph's life he saw victories turn to defeat. He experienced disappointment with people. He was imprisoned without cause and lied about by those over him. It was thirteen long years before the God-given dream came to pass in his life.

The sufferings of Joseph, the dreamer, are recounted in Psalm 105:16-19. Verse 19 ends with this summary: "The word of the Lord tested him." Every dreamer will be tested and afflicted by those around him and even by God Himself. As the preacher observes in Ecclesiastes 5:3, "The dream comes through much effort."

A World War II army slogan said, "The difficult we do immediately; the impossible takes a little longer." Is your dream difficult or even impossible? If it's difficult, the fulfillment might take a while. If it's impossible, it might take a little longer! Are you ready to see it through?

Make a covenant with yourself not to give up in times of discouragement, frustration or pressure. Tell yourself that going back or quitting are not options. Unite yourself with people who are going in the same direction. Encourage each other toward the goal. Search out dreamers who have paid the price to make their dreams come to pass.

Step-by-Step

3. You must chart your course scripturally and practically. "By wisdom a house is built, and by understanding it is established; and by knowledge the rooms are filled" (Prov. 24:3,4). The sense of this passage is that planning is essential to bring our dreams to fruition.

You must have a plan! You must know what you want in order to create faith for the target and move toward it. Otherwise, as someone once said, "Blessed is he who aims at nothing, for he shall succeed."

Do you have a target? Is the target set before you in such a way that you understand all the steps that must be taken in order to hit it? Have you charted a course to reach it? To discover new oceans and unseen land beyond the horizon you must first let the shoreline disappear from sight behind you.

I know a writer who was intrigued by ordinary people who stepped out and charted their dreams. In fact, he kept a "dreamer's file" filled with newspaper clippings about them. For example, there were the two Voyager pilots who invested their savings and bet their lives on a dream born from doodlings on a restaurant napkin in 1981.

"What kind of world would there be," these two asked, "if there were no daring?" They dreamed big dreams and plotted a course that eventually took them into the cramped cockpit of an experimental airplane on a non-stop flight around the world.

God loves planners. He respects people who think enough of their dreams to create plans to attain them. Noah had a plan for the ark. Moses had a plan for the tabernacle and motivated other people to help him build it. David and Solomon had a plan for the temple and motivated many to help them build this great house for God.

To have a plan is to be wise, and God loves wise people. Realistic goals help you measure your progress. Without a plan and specific goals, you'll wander aimlessly. And you'll never fulfill your dreams.

At the Helm

4. You must stay on course. The helmsman is the one in charge of steering a ship. The ship is directed according to his knowledge of the course that has been charted.

God has given you a course, and you are the helmsman. You work in conjunction with the Holy Spirit to manage the plan God has given you. You must stay on course at all costs.

Hard winds will try to drive your ship off course. You'll encounter clouds, fog, icebergs, sudden storms and shallow water with hidden rocks, all trying to ruin your ship or to put you off course. But a wise helmsman charts his course carefully, studies the clouds and knows how to handle his ship in the fog. He uses the technical machinery available to him to spot the icebergs under the water that the eye cannot see. He expects sudden storms and is therefore always ready. Shallow water is not new to him. He looks for the hidden reefs and knows to steer away from them.

Five Obstacles

If you want to stay on course, you too must know the obstacles and steer your ship accordingly. You must learn to deal with five obstacles in particular:

The first obstacle is you. The important word here is *discipline*. Discipline is doing what doesn't come naturally. Though it's hard, it's the key to taking charge of your life. Discipline includes ''won't power,'' which is just as important as ''will power.'' You need to decide what you won't do, what you won't give in to and what you won't waste your time on.

A second obstacle is your past. This may include failed plans, ruined dreams, aborted goals, what others have said to you, or anything else in your past that's weighing you down. You must not let the past determine your future. The past is past! Put it behind you by the power and blood of Jesus.

A third obstacle is your resources. God uses money to teach us and to direct us. When we have no resources, we think we have no options. Don't let lack of financial resources abort your dreams. You have educational resources, spiritual resources and, yes, financial resources—all of which you must channel properly in order to fulfill your dream.

A fourth obstacle is your frame of reference. Enlarge your frame of reference by enlarging your reading habits. Read about great men and women of God who did great things and who understood how to think big.

If you stay around people who think small, your frame of reference will shrink. But if you study the Bible, meditate on the Word of God and walk with others who do the same, your frame of reference will grow. You'll understand that God can and will do the impossible with those who are willing to take risks.

The fifth obstacle is what I call the "3-D obstacle": disappointments, discouragement and delays. If you can pass the 3-D test, you'll fulfill your dreams and visions.

Disappointment comes to everyone—disappointment in ourselves, in people around us and sometimes even in God.

Discouragement also happens to everyone. Have you ever been so discouraged that, like David, you concluded that you would just die? David thought that Saul would take his life, but, in fact, Saul didn't take his life. David became king. But in a moment of discouragement David couldn't see God's plan.

Delays are simply part of life. They can cause you to misinterpret what God is trying to do. But God's timing is different from human timing. So one key to fulfilling your dream is to be patient and allow God to work out what He wants to do, the way He wants to do it.

The Art of Finishing

5. You must finish your course. Henry Wadsworth Longfellow once said, "Great is the art of beginning, but greater the art of finishing." Paul knew what it was to finish: "I have fought the good fight," he said, "I have finished the course, I have kept the faith" (2 Tim. 4:7).

Paul describes three people later on in 2 Timothy 4 who began their course with good intentions. But only two of them reached the finish line.

The first is Demas. Paul writes, "For Demas, having loved this present world, has deserted me and gone to Thessalonica" (verse 10). Demas was surrounded by strong men. He began but he never finished. He saw with his eyes the dream of fulfilling his ministry with Paul, but he was never able to say, "I have finished my course, I have kept the faith." Demas's heart changed. His dream faded because of testing and obstacles.

Restored After a Stumble

In verse 11 Paul refers to another man who was a dreamer: ''Pick up Mark and bring him with you, for he is useful to me for service.'' Mark was a man who turned failure into triumph, disaster into destiny. He was restored after a stumbling.

Mark was the young man who deserted Paul because of some hardships during one of the missionary journeys. Barnabas, the encourager, talked Paul into giving Mark a second chance. This time Mark came back to finish his course in the face of failure and ridicule. What an honor for Paul to record his name in the Bible with the comment, ''Bring this young man to me; he is useful in the ministry.''

Maybe you, like Mark, have failed before. Maybe the past is still before you. You look at yourself and say, I'm not sure I can fulfill my dreams. If so, be a Mark, not a Demas! Don't give up now. God has called you to be a dreamer who finishes his or her course.

Great Lion of God

The third person described in this chapter is Paul himself. Verses 5 through 8 tell of this great lion of God who had a dream, paid the price for it and made it come to pass. Paul's secret strength, which enabled him to finish the course, is then revealed in verses 17 and 18:

But the Lord stood with me, and strengthened me, in order that through me the proclamation might be fully accomplished, and that all the Gentiles might hear; and I was delivered out of the lion's mouth. The Lord will deliver me from every evil deed, and will bring me safely to His heavenly kingdom; to Him be the glory forever and ever. Amen.

NOTES

Chapter 1

1. Paul Lee Tan, *The Encyclopedia of 7700 Illustrations* (Rockville, Md.: Assurance Publishers, 1979), p. 1469.

Chapter 3

2. Herbert Lockyer, *All the Promises of the Bible* (Grand Rapids, Mich.: Zondervan Publishing House, 1962), p. 55.

Chapter 4

3. Quoted in *Motivation to Last a Lifetime* by Ted W. Engstrom (with Robert C. Larson) (Grand Rapids, Mich.: Zondervan Publishing House, 1984), p. 43.

4. Quoted in Engstrom, p. 11.

Chapter 8

5. James Dobson, *Parenting Isn't for Cowards* (Waco, Tex.: Word Publications, Inc., 1987).

6. James Dobson, "It's Never Too Late to Change," *Focus on the Family* magazine (Pomona, Calif.); used with permission.